Rude

Contemporary Black Canadian Cultural Criticism

Other books by the editor

Black Like Who?:Writing Black Canada

Rude

Contemporary Black Canadian Cultural Criticism

edited by Rinaldo Walcott

INSOMNIAC PRESS

Copyright © 2000 by Rinaldo Walcott

All rights reserved. No part of this publication may be reproduced, stored in a retrieval system or transmitted, in any form or by any means, without the prior written permission of the publisher or, in the case of photocopying or other reprographic copying, a licence from CANCOPY (Canadian Copyright Licensing Agency), 1 Yonge St., Suite 1900, Toronto, Ontario, Canada, M5E 1E5.

Edited by Rinaldo Walcott
Copy edited by Maria Lundin
Designed by Mike O'Connor

Canadian Cataloguing in Publication Data

Main entry under title:

Rude: contemporary Black Canadian cultural criticism

Includes index.
ISBN 1-895837-74-X

1. Black Canadians - Social life and customs.* I.Walcott, Rinaldo
   Black Studies, Cultural Studies, Literary Studies.

FC106.B6R82 2000   305.896'071   C00-930469-X
F1035.N3R82 2000

The publisher gratefully acknowledges the support of the Canada Council, the Ontario Arts Council and Department of Canadian Heritage through the Book Publishing Industry Development Program.

THE CANADA COUNCIL | LE CONSEIL DES ARTS
FOR THE ARTS | DU CANADA
SINCE 1957 | DEPUIS 1957

Printed and bound in Canada

ONTARIO ARTS
COUNCIL
CONSEIL DES ARTS
DE L'ONTARIO

Insomniac Press, 192 Spadina Avenue, Suite 403,
Toronto, Ontario, Canada, M5T 2C2
www.insomniacpress.com

Table of contents

By Way of a Brief Introduction
Insubordination: A Demand
for a Different Canada

Rude: Contemporary Black Canadian Cultural Criticism takes it title from at least two signifying moments. First, Clement Virgo's film *Rude* (1995) opened up the space for thinking differently about Canada as a racialized space, and more specifically, a Black space. While that opening brought with it certain kinds of limitations in how it imagined Blackness in Canada, the opening signalled, along with a number of other openings in literature, theatre, music, visual arts and a range of other creative arts, a take on Canada that has required a fresh look at Blackness here. Second, *Rude*, the anthology, intends to undermine or at least trouble notions of the nation — that is, the Canadian nation-state — when it encounters a self-assured Blackness. In this sense, *Rude* is an engaged insubordination with respect to official narrative discourses of the nation-state of Canada. Collected here are a group of rebellious essays, which attempt to say something about the nation's encounters with Blackness. These encounters between Blackness and nation see neither as sacred, innocent nor free from critical engagement and debate — indeed, in some cases, harsh critique.

The founding narratives of Canada leave little, if any room for imagining Blackness as constitutive of Canadianness. While Black people date their presence in Canada from as early as the 1600s, Blackness is still considered a recent phenomenon within the nation. This problem of thinking Blackness as recent means that long-standing Black communities across the nation continually have their presence absented in the founding narrative of the nation. And yet these long-standing communities find ways to resist this erasure in their personal, collective and everyday histories. The founding narrative of the nation, in its attempt to give credence to Francophone and Anglophone needs, also occludes Aboriginal peoples. But this nation of ours does not admit to this exclusion easily; instead, it must continually demonstrate its benevolence and tolerance. So both Aboriginals and Others are imagined in the nation in very specific and proscribed ways. In fact, acts of legislation such as the *Indian Act* and the *Multiculturalism Act* are the ways in which these groups are reimagined in the nation. Their not-quite-citizen status presents an interesting dilemma. Some of the essays in *Rude* suggest that this not-quite-citizen status is one reason why it is necessary to be insubordinate to the nation. This insubordination is not merely an infantile rebellion but rather a different relation to the narratives of nation, which seek to subordinate Blackness as merely adjunct to the "real" and more sustaining national story.

One of the first things any reader will notice about the essays is that their principle impetus is not to prove that racism exists. The essayists take racism as a given in the Canadian social and cultural landscape. Rather, these essayists are interested in mapping out the ways in which intra-Black dialogues reframe the nation. They ask us to consider our perceptions of the nation and how Black people within the nation make, what Paul Gilroy calls, stories of "love and loss." The essayists, then, refuse the too-heavy "socio-logic" category of anti-racism and instead enter the much messier terrain of cultural politics. Thus, the writers attempt to render the terms through which representations can become more visible and complex. At stake for the essayists is: In the name of what do representations matter? Under what terms do specific representations become official representations? How do representations produce community, citizens and, ultimately, a nation? What is the ethical dimension of various representations and how does one ethically respond to them? What is the politics that informs specific representations? These questions animate the essays collected in *Rude*.

In 1999, the Rascalz, a Canadian rap group, performed for the first time in the prime time segment of the Juno Awards. The Rascalz had refused their Juno the previous year (1998) in what they termed a protest against the fact that Urban music (the new code for Black music) was not supported enough in the Canadian context despite its saleability. I find two things interesting about the Rascalz and the politics of their refusal. The song from the album they were nominated for, "Northern Touches," was a collaboration between the Vancouver-based rappers and some Toronto-based rappers. This collaboration signalled for me a Black remapping of the Canadian landscape because these rappers (and rappers are normally highly sensitive to issues of geographic space: city, neighbourhood, et cetera) refused the binary opposition of east coast/west coast in their collaborative effort. This effort was not merely about refusing the Canadian geographic imaginary, however; it was also about refusing the all too media-saturated coverage of an east coast/west coast split among African American rappers, characterized by the high-profile deaths of Tupac Shakur and Notorious B.I.G. or Biggie Smalls. Canadian rappers in one sonic track repositioned both national and international discourses of Blackness, in what I call a creative insubordination. Second, the appearance of the Rascalz in the prime time segment of the Juno's brought to centre stage a self-assured Blackness. This Blackness was so self-assured that it could refuse its Juno of the previous year. And while the Rascalz were not able to muster any profound statements about their historic appearance, they at least gestured to its significance. The Rascalz most recent album *Global Warning* (1999) continues this self-assurance, as the title suggests that they are ready to take the world by storm with their Canadian-inflected rap. The Rascalz represent the changed relations of Blackness in Canada, showing that representations of thinking within and against the nation are necessary and vital to the projects of a whole host of Black Canadian artists working across many genres.

Self-assuredness brings with it a particular kind of insubordination. It requires that one be aware of the various kinds of relations that serve to place subjects in subordinate positions. The essays in *Rude* analyze a range of creative insubordinations. But the essays are also insubordinate themselves, because they do not merely read texts as innocent or somehow outside the political realm. In fact the essays are keenly aware of the ways in which texts can be both political and simultaneously inserted into existing, normative discourses. For example, essays by Peter Hudson, Renuka Sooknanan and Leslie Sanders highlight the political efficacy of specific texts or events and their meaning for questions of Black community, citizenship and modes of belonging to the nation. In other essays, Richard Almonte, Rinaldo Walcott and David Sealy address how texts and narratives of the nation present specific appearances of Blackness even while those same narratives seek to render Blackness a void in the Canadian polity. These essays attempt to fill the "Black hole" with a Black Canadian agency that extends beyond the clutches of racism and victimhood. Joy Mannette, Tess Chakkalakal, Gamel Abdel Shehid and Awad Ibrahim all demonstrate how one comes into Blackness in Canada through a series of social and cultural markings, that give substance to Blackness in Canada. These essays ask us to think about how the terms of Blackness are both taken on as affirmative and resisted as oppressive. All the essays in *Rude* seek to unmask and make urgently present mechanisms and conceptual tools available for discussing and thinking about Blackness in Canada without sentimentality. These essays are neither celebratory nor dismissive. Rather they take the various discourses of Blackness in Canada seriously in order to inaugurate a wide-ranging conversation on Blackness and therefore Black peoples in Canada.

Finally, the essays in this collection put to bed the lie that thinking about Blackness in Canada is but a recent phenomenon. In fact, some of the contributors in the collection have been writing about Blackness in Canada for many years. Some others have written dissertations on Blackness in Canada, and still others are in the process of writing dissertations on Blackness in Canada. (The myth that scholarship on Blackness is recent is parallel to the myth of Blackness as recent in the nation — and must be resisted with the same force.) These essays speak to the "new" self-assuredness of Black scholarship in Canada. That this scholarship crosses race, gender and ethnic lines and comes from a multiplicity of class origins is also important. One weakness of this anthology is that as editor I was not able to acquire any work on Black queer subjectivity in Canada. In spite of the latter shortcoming (and a serious one it is) this politically engaged scholarship seeks to complicate and push the boundaries of racial designation, but also the boundaries of the academic responses to Blackness within Canada. The essays in *Rude* — the provisional text that it is — seek to break out of the dreary doldrums of scholarship on Blackness in Canada and move beyond the confines of the assumption that only a few qualified speakers exist. All ten of the essayists in *Rude* are but the tip the iceberg. The real political issue is when will those who shape the dominant cultural taste of the Canadian imaginary deal seriously with the apparent outpouring of contemporary Black Canadian expressive culture? *Rude* attempts to provoke such a conversation. It is a modest response to the emergence of what we might call a new Black Canadian politicality that derives its sense of self from living life at the in-between but not being bothered by that condition. In fact the in-between is a source for making demands of the nation and, when necessary, jettisoning the nation to make necessary international or diasporic connections. It is in this sense that the essays in *Rude* demand a different and more ethical Canada.

"Treason in the Fort":
Blackness and Canadian Literature

Richard Almonte

The impetus behind this essay comes from two directions. The first is typically academic, while the second is not. The initial impetus is the traditional academic need to respond to someone else's work. Published in the Spring 1999 issue of *Essays on Canadian Writing*, "In Praise of Talking Dogs: The Study and Teaching of Early Canada's Canonless Canon," Nick Mount, argues against the validity of early Canadian literature as a worthy field of academic study and teaching. The author's conclusion is radical and seductive: early Canadian literature does not exist because there are no texts worthy enough to constitute it. The author of the present essay feels an affinity for the author of the polemic essay. They are both doctoral candidates, and specialize in early Canadian literature, which puts them in a small enough group. Moreover, both have obviously questioned the validity of early Canadian literature as an area of academic specialty. The present author decides that a considered response to Mount's essay is a worthwhile and necessary project; and responses to polemical arguments tend to create a whiff of controversy.

The second impetus behind this essay is thoroughly lacking in premeditation. Before being able to write a considered response to Mount's essay, this author faces studying for his Special Area Examinations in Canadian literature at McMaster University. Although his area of research is in little-known Black Canadian writing from the nineteenth century, his examination will be based on a more recognizable, more canonical list of Canadian literature, from Richardson and Moodie, through Callaghan and MacLennan, to Ondaatje and Atwood. As the exam date looms closer, he begins to think he does not have enough time to study for the exams in addition to writing a worthy response to Mount. He does not expect to find any correlation between his reading of canonical Canadian literature and his research in marginalized early Black Canadian writing. He assumes incorrectly, however. As he makes his way through his reading list, this author finds that many Canadian works considered canonical also deal with Blackness. He decides that writing an essay in response to Mount is, in fact, a good way to study for his exams. The thesis of this essay is simple: Black characters and Blackness are substantive, not peripheral, components of nineteenth and early twentieth-century Canadian literature. As a result, Mount's thesis that there is little worth reading and teaching can be rejected, since at least one worthwhile thing has been uncovered: a long-standing fascination with Blackness within early Canadian literature.

In order to lend credence to the argument that Blackness is a worthy enough reason to revalue early Canadian literature, the logic deployed in Mount's essay to devalue early Canadian literature needs to be scrutinized more closely. Following this, I will offer an examination of a well-known example of the type of work this essay seeks to accomplish, Toni Morrison's *Playing in the Dark: Whiteness and the Literary Imagination*. Morrison's theory of the discernible function of Blackness in white American literature serves as both a guide for this essay and as a catalyst for further theorizing, since the situation in American literature is not exactly parallel to its corresponding Canadian field. Finally, this essay considers four canonical works of early Canadian literature: *Wacousta*, *The Clockmaker*, *Roughing it in the Bush*, and *Les anciens Canadiens*, as well as one work from the mid-twentieth century, Callaghan's *The Loved and the Lost*. These works were chosen for three reasons: first, to differing degrees, they are all interested in Blackness; second, they or their authors are canonical, and therefore define the country's literary culture; and finally, they are all eminently enjoyable, which appears to be Mount's overriding concern when it comes to deciding what can and cannot be deemed literature.

The guiding premise of Mount's essay is that a binary opposition exists within criticism of early Canadian literature between evaluative criticism and nonevaluative criticism. Mount valorizes evaluative criticism because it doesn't pull punches: the critic dares to state opinions about what is good and what is not good. Mount's crisis stems from the fact that, as a proponent of evaluative criticism, he finds himself a specialist in a field he considers woefully lacking in good books. Mount criticizes nonevaluative criticism because it is not authentic to what he sees as the true work of the academic. For Mount, nonevaluative criticism is synonymous with cultural studies, and cultural studies is concerned with concepts like race and gender. According to Mount, the scales are currently tipped in favour of the latter type of criticism:

> Of the thirty-six articles published in the last five years on pre-World War I Canadian literature, not one is concerned to evaluate the literary merits of the text or texts that it reads (77).

This fact is buttressed by the alarming realization that "the reigning figure in the Works Cited list of current Canadian criticism is not F.R. Leavis but Homi K. Bhabha" (78). Mount's argument is neatly summarized near the end of his essay, when he writes that there is a "tendency to value the nineteenth-century Canadian text more for what it says (or can be made to say) about a cultural-historical phenomenon than for its literary merits" (88).

Where to begin to build the case against Mount? Do we interrogate the note of paranoia that lurks behind his notion that considerations of race and gender are antithetical to the work an English department? Or do we ask whether Mount's neat opposition of evaluative versus nonevaluative criticism actually holds up in practice? In fact, a good place to begin is with Mount's undefended assumption of a universally acceptable definition of what is good. In a number of instances, Mount carefully shows that various works considered part of the early Canadian literature canon, such as the diary of David Thompson, are just plain bad.[1] In the case of Thompson, Mount sets the bad Canadian example against a good American example, Thoreau, and asks the reader to decide for him or herself whether or not Thompson is an important writer. Mount's arsenal includes close textual analyses of badly written passages, as well as extra-literary evidence, such as enrollment statistics gleaned from English departments across the country which suggest that early Canadian literature courses are not very popular.

An example from a nineteenth-century Canadian text of which

Mount would probably disapprove may help clear things up. Mary Shadd, an American immigrant to Canada, published *A Plea For Emigration* in 1852. The book contains an astounding declaration in the following section, where Shadd discusses the sort of help American Blacks are sending the fugitive slaves in Canada:

> Individuals in the United States often send books to those most needy, yet they are usually of such a character as to be utterly useless. I have often thought if it is really a benevolent act to send...old novels, and all manner of obsolete books to them... Why not give, when gifts are needed, of that which is useful? (67)

An argument that Mount has probably not considered concerns the utility of literature. Mount may not like immigrant guides and exploration narratives and other less-than-good literature, but by holding that opinion, might he be overlooking what was considered good during the very period in which he has specialized? Instead of mourning the absence of the Canadian Poe, the Canadian Hawthorne or the Canadian Dickinson, why not deal with what is here? Can we not be evaluative and still decide that what is here is good?

There are other methodologies with which such a challenge can be mounted. Toni Morrison's *Playing in the Dark: Whiteness and the Literary Imagination* rereads canonical nineteenth-century and early twentieth-century American Literature, ascribing value to writers such as Poe, Twain, Cather, and Hemingway, not primarily because of the literariness of their writing — although this too is taken into consideration — but mainly because of the degree to which these authors and their texts engage with Blackness. Morrison argues that the characteristics traditionally "championed" in the "national literature...are...in fact responses to a dark, abiding, signing Africanist presence" (5). For Morrison, the presence of Blackness in white American writing is straightforward: "the subject of the dream is the dreamer. The fabrication of an Africanist persona is...an extraordinary meditation on the self...of the fears and desires that reside in the writerly consciousness" (17). Morrison's criticism of the American canon is eminently utilitarian. She shows how literature has meaning and value for reasons that lie outside the traditional, aesthetic criteria championed by Mount.

In Morrison's theory, American fiction is populated by Black characters whose presence performs a specific function. The "duties" of these characters are "duties of exorcism and reification and mirroring" and they help to "form the distinguishing characteristics of a proto-American literature"(39). Morrison provides a taxonomy of stock plots and linguistic strategies whereby the reader can see the Black character performing these duties. One common stock plot is the use of a Black character's story as a "means of meditation"(53) on the humanity of a white character, as in *Huckleberry Finn*. A stock linguistic strategy is the use of what Morrison calls an "economy of stereotype,"(67) and she shows how this works in her reading of Hemingway's *To Have and Have Not* (70-76). That Morrison is successful in her rewriting of the accepted narrative of American literary history is not in question. The usefulness of her approach to the quite different Canadian context needs, however, to be explained.

Morrison's argument is a new way of looking at what is a well-established paradigm of American literary history. Beginning with works like F.O. Matthiessen's *American Romance*, the idea that American literature is dominated by themes of "individuality, masculinity [and] social engagement"(5) is still entrenched, despite feminist and other interventions. Beginning with this idea, Morrison is to propose a theory based on doubling, on mirrors, where the literary character looks inside himself or herself and sees a Black image staring back at him. In the Canadian context, however, which has been theorized as antithetical to individuality, masculinity, and social engagement, how do we account for the strong presence of ideas around Blackness?[2] Northrop Frye's seminal essay in *The Literary History of Canada* (1965) continues to resonate as the most creative summation of the development of early Canadian literature. Frye famously proposes his "garrison mentality"(342) theory, which sees early Canadian writers as obsessed by the re-creation of community, as well as by the xenophobic fear of all threats from outside it.

Perhaps the best place to begin to examine the uses of Blackness in canonical Canadian literature is with John Richardson's *Wacousta* (1832). This gothic romance — albeit indebted to the American James Fenimore Cooper's earlier adventure romances for its swift-moving plot and its generic characterization — nonetheless succeeds in inaugurating something completely un-American, a literature that insists on the importance of community. The garrison at Fort Detroit, where the action of the novel is centred, continues to be read as a microcosm of English, and later, Canadian, society.[3] The hierarchical nature of this society is underscored by the fact that the novel deals with the daily running of a military fort. The military's strict rules and rigid structure are in evidence from the beginning of the novel, as Richardson describes in detail the "cautious discipline established in the fort"(19). The appeal of the novel, stems from the fact that while the garrison community appears to function smoothly along hierarchical lines, it is in fact also the locus of many discontents that fly directly in the face of this studied discipline.

Two of these discontents are present at the beginning of the novel, in the form of Ellen Halloway, wife of the accused Frank Halloway, who interrupts her husband's court martial twice. Ellen's actions raise the ire of the fort's Governor, de Haldimar, which he expresses in a statement heavy with ideological meaning: "I desire that, in future…the women of the regiment may be kept out of the way. Look to it sir!"(40). Women, we find as we read further in the novel, are a silenced part of the garrison community. Disturbing the garrison's smooth running is also the presence of class antagonisms, for example, in a conversation between Lieutenant Murphy and Captain Blessington. Murphy, whose ethnicity and class are clearly marked by Richardson's use of a substandard English when recording his conversation, eagerly anticipates his promotion to Lieutenant. His eagerness is curtly dismissed by Blessington, who predicts that those who anticipate this sort of promotion so eagerly may be "the first to be cut off" (27). The end of the chapter gruesomely enacts Blessington's prediction when Murphy is killed.

The presence of a Black character in the first chapter provides a third example of how the garrison is internally divided. The servant Sambo appears right at the end of the highly dramatic second chapter. He is introduced in an overdetermined and contradictory fashion by one of the soldiers. Blessington asks Erskine if he has heard anything (an intruder has just escaped from the fort). Erskine replies: "'Not a sound ourselves, but here is Sir Everard's black servant, Sambo, who has just riveted our attention, by declaring that *he* distinctly heard a groan towards the skirt of the common.'"(28) Sambo's appearance is contradictory: while his colour and race are foregrounded ("black servant"), he is also granted authority by virtue of being able to hear things that the regular soldiers do not. Sambo thus rivets the soldiers' attention, yet Richardson is unclear as to whether this is because of Sambo's colour or because of his precise hearing capabilities. This contradictory Blackness is further manifested by Sambo's actions. "Sambo, quick, my rifle," Sir Everard says, and Sambo does as he is told, "unbidden...as if tutored to the task"(29). Sambo is a dutiful servant. At the same time, the two lines of dialogue Sambo is given by Richardson betray the former's impatience with duty: "Make haste, massa...Sambo see him get up,"(29) Sambo tells Sir Everard as he points his musket at the enemy in the distance. And a moment later, "Quick, quick, massa — him quite up,"(30) is Sambo's impatient advice to his master, who is beginning to look incompetent next to his own "boy"(30). Fulfilling this subtle upsetting of the master-servant balance, Sir Everard blames Sambo — "You scoundrel, it was all your fault — you moved your shoulder as I pulled the trigger"(30) — when he fails to hit the enemy. The internal presence of Blackness, along with other "threats," such as the presence of women and class distinctions, plunges the garrison into turmoil.

A Black servant makes a conspicuous appearance in another canonical work of early Canadian literature, Thomas Haliburton's *The Clockmaker* (1836). In the sketch, "Fire in the Dairy," Sam Slick tells the Judge about his visit with Marm Blake. Walking into the room where Marm Blake sits by her fire, Slick notes the presence of a "black heifer in the corner"(137). This is Beck, Squire and Marm Blake's servant. Haliburton's propensity for having Slick compare Blacks to animals is clear in this sketch, as is his consistent use of the stereotype of the Black servant as a figure of comic relief. It seems that Beck can do nothing right. Marm Blake accuses her of being "def as a post"(137) and then Slick notes that Beck's sweeping raises "such an awful thick cloud o'dust" that he doesn't know if he will "ever see or breathe...ag'in"(137). The final joke of the sketch sees Beck screaming that "there's Fire in the dairy"(138). Slick assumes this means a fire, but it turns out that Fire is the name of Blake's dog. Slick follows Beck into the dairy, assuming he will be putting out a fire, but instead he proceeds to push Beck into the swill-tub by accident. Marm Blake, like Sir Everard in *Wacousta*, blames her Black servant for the upsetting events: "you good-for-nothin' hussy; that's all your carelessness,"(138) when we know that the Black servant is not to blame.

Roughly one third of the thirty-three sketches in the first series of *The Clockmaker* contain some reference to Black characters, often called "niggers"(17). This abundance of references has not gone unnoticed. Both George Elliott Clarke and Dieter Meindl have written about Haliburton's use of Black characters.[4] While both of these critics rightly point to the racist nature of Haliburton's portrayals, they do not place these portrayals in the larger context of early Canadian literature. In fact, Haliburton's use of Blackness is more subtle than Clarke and Meindl would have us believe. In the sketch "The White Nigger," Haliburton grasps the essential paradox (identified by Morrison also) that has marred the American political and social landscape for centuries. That country is founded on principles of freedom whereas in practice it "tolerates...slavery in its worst and most forbidding form"(131). Haliburton's satire is so subtle that he follows (and likens) this condemnation of American slavery with a sketch, "Fire in the Dairy," that provides a detailed picture of the mistreatment of a Black Canadian servant by her white Canadian mistress. In a more direct way than John Richardson before him, and using satire rather than romance, Haliburton points to Blackness as a troubling element in the emerging Canadian community.

Following Richardson and Haliburton, Susanna Moodie draws her own picture of a Canadian community and its response to the presence of Blackness. Published in 1852, *Roughing it in the Bush* appears two years after the passage of the American Fugitive Slave Law, which resulted in thousands of Black American emigrants and escaped slaves passing over the borders of Michigan and New York into Canada West. Although set a decade and a half earlier, around the Rebellion of 1837, at least one of Moodie's sketches of Upper Canadian life appears to refer prophetically to the future passing of the Fugitive Slave Law. "The Charivari," whose ostensible subject is the quaint Canadian custom, inherited from Quebec, of taunting mismatched couples on their wedding night, turns into an examination of white Canadian settlers' sentiments towards Black people.

The sketch begins with Mrs. Moodie asking Mrs. O– for an explanation of the meaning of the word "charivari." Mrs. O– proceeds to explain that it is a "queer custom" where "all the idle young fellows in the neighbourhood...disguise themselves, blackening their faces"(221) in order to play pranks on unfortunate newlyweds. The results are more serious than most pranks, however. In a suspiciously contradictory manner, Mrs. O– relates to Mrs. Moodie the story of Tom Smith:

'There was a runaway nigger… came to the village, and set up a barber's poll, and settled among us. I am no friend to the blacks; but really Tom Smith was such a quiet, good-natured fellow…that he soon got a good business… Well, after a time he persuaded a white girl to marry him. She was a not bad-looking Irish woman, and I can't think what bewitched the creature to take him'(224).

The contradictions here — Tom as a "runaway nigger" but also a "good-natured fellow," and the "not bad-looking Irish woman" who yet is "bewitched" enough to marry a Black man — point to a larger and more troubling notion. The idle young fellows of the town, who dress up in blackface, end up murdering the Black man: "they so ill-treated" Tom Smith, "that he died under their hands"(224). These sons of "respectable families"(224) use borrowed Blackness as their license to commit crime, and find a victim for their crime in a Black man.

Mrs. Moodie's disgust at this story barely has time to register with the reader before another neighbour, Mrs. D–, appears on the scene, once again disparaging Black people. For the second time in one sketch, Moodie carefully portrays an instance of racial hatred with the ironic fact of a white character taking on colour. Mrs. D– takes offense at Mrs. Moodie's defense of Mollineux, a Black servant: "Indeed!" Mrs. Moodie argues, "Is he not the same flesh and blood as the rest?"(227) The next sentence is vital: "The colour rose into Mrs. D–'s sallow face, and she answered, with much warmth, "What! Do you mean to compare *me* with a *nigger*!"(227) Moodie's description of Mrs. D– and her rising colour has, of course, already made the comparison explicit. The question remains, what is Moodie saying with her ironic pointing out of the fact that whiteness so easily becomes Blackness?

In the last of our canonical early Canadian works, Philippe Aubert de Gaspé's *Les anciens Canadiens* (1864), Blackness is an important force, even though within the plot of the novel it appears in only one episode, and in a single character, the servant Lisette. Aubert de Gaspé's novel is a foundational text in Quebec literature, but its overtly political message — that the French must learn to get along in an English-led society — has not always been popular. Set in the years leading up to the war between England and France for control of New France, *Les anciens Canadiens* portrays a society that is as rigidly stratified as that of *Wacousta*. When introducing the main characters of the novel, for instance, the narrator claims that "il est juste de les introduire suivant leur rang hiérarchique"(122). Internal family hierarchy is a figure for the national and racial hierarchies that exist outside the symbolic manor house of the d'Haberville family. These hierarchies are manifest in the relationship between the French Canadian d'Haberville family, their British friend Archibald Cameron of Locheill, and the many Indian tribes and nations that appear throughout the novel. The Blackness in this novel exists, importantly, in the kitchen of the French Canadian manor house, the symbolic centre of the novel's action.

Lisette, a servant of the d'Haberville family, appears towards the end of the novel. We learn, to our surprise, that one of the main characters in the novel, Jules, has been raised by a Black woman, "la mulatresse Lisette"(271). The novel's earlier stress on the d'Haberville family, and the division of responsibilities within that family, recedes upon the appearance of Lisette, whom Archibald, the Scottish hero of this novel, makes a point of visiting after the war is over. As we shall see, the subtle linking of the British hero with the Black woman is a deliberate move on Aubert de Gaspé's part. Lisette begins her service in the d'Haberville household as a slave: "le capitaine [l'] avait achetée à l'age de quatre ans"(272). Even though she is a slave, Aubert de Gaspé assures his readers that Lisette actually pays very little heed to what her master desires, and almost none to her mistress: "quant à la maîtresse...elle ne lui obéissait qu'en temps et lieux"(272). Aubert de Gaspé's stereotypical rendering of Lisette as the happy slave is all the more incredible when we find out that even though the d'Haberville family has officially freed Lisette, she doesn't think too much of this freedom: "'se moquait de son émancipation'"(272). The contradictory portrayal of Lisette, at once emancipated servant and "pauvre esclave"(272) points towards the allegorical reading Aubert de Gaspé intends. Lisette is to the d'Haberville family as the French Canadians should be to their new British captors. Thus, the British hero's instinctive empathy for Lisette can be read as the narrator's recognition of submission and cooperation.

In the final work to be considered, Callaghan's *The Loved and the Lost* (1951), the colonial sensibility of the four early Canadian works is absent; Canadian literature has by the fifties donned the guise of Modernism. The descriptive writing that characterizes the four earlier works gives way to a dialogue-driven prose where the few descriptive passages are pointedly symbolic. Montreal, that city so eminently suitable to geographic symbolism, is at the heart of Callaghan's novel. Unlike the earlier works, this novel is specifically written to address the relationship between Blacks and whites in Canada. The novel takes place in Montreal where the "whiteness of the snowbound city" is in constant opposition to the "black barrier of the mountain"(67). White and Black recur in this novel, both as features of the landscape, and as features of the plot. Jim McAlpine, the hero of the novel, falls in love with Peggy Sanderson, a white woman who is in turn attracted to the Blackness she finds in Montreal's St. Antoine neighbourhood: Black writing, Black nightclubs, and Black men. Ultimately, the tragic irony of the novel is that the only white person who understands Peggy's attraction to Blackness — Jim — cannot save her from being destroyed by this same attraction.

The problem Blackness causes in Callaghan's Montreal is more acute than in the communities of the earlier works. A number of white characters who profess to be racially unprejudiced are shown to be false. At the beginning of the novel, Peggy, Jim, and his friend Chuck discuss Black writing. Jim claims that "some of these Negro writers are pretty good," to which his friend Chuck responds with calculated sarcasm, "Sure," he says "don't we all like them?"(18) In the racially charged Montreal Callaghan portrays, the explanation given for Peggy's attraction to Blackness becomes crucial. She explains to Jim that a childhood incident where she stumbles upon a naked Black boy on a beach, and is transfixed by his beauty, has caused her attraction to Blackness. Peggy's childhood awareness — prompted by her encounter with Blackness — that "beauty could be painful"(45) is a subtle foreshadowing of her tragic end. Despised and betrayed by both the white community and her adopted Black community, Peggy's sad fate closes a deeply pessimistic novel. Not even Callaghan's self-conscious and satirical use of Stowe's *Uncle Tom's Cabin* (74) and Kipling's "White Man's Burden"(125) can hide the fact that *The Loved and the*

Lost posits a society where Blackness is seen as dangerous and forbidden.

The title of the present essay borrows a phrase — "treason in the fort" — from Richardson's *Wacousta*. If the "fort," after Frye, is a euphemism for the Canadian community, then "treason in the fort" is an apt way of describing the presence of Blackness in fictional Canadian communities. Treason is betrayal from within, and as we have seen in our brief readings of Richardson, Haliburton, Moodie, de Gaspé, and Callaghan, Blackness is treasonous. In examples as varied as the unreliability of the servants, Sambo, Beck and Lisette; and the beguiling attraction Blackness has on white characters, as with the some of the settlers in *Roughing It In the Bush*, or Peggy and Jim in *The Loved and the Lost*, the common denominator is that Blackness is a threat to the status quo of white Canadian community. Morrison's injunction that Blackness in white-authored American literature is by definition "reflexive"(17) must be changed, in the Canadian context, to "defensive." Blackness signals not so much what whites might be, as what they do not want to be.

That a detectable and heretofore ignored Black presence should permeate works as different as the five discussed here is a valid and instructive enough reason to reject Mount's claims that early Canadian literature is not very good. It depends, in the end, where you choose to look.

Works Cited

Aubert de Gaspé, Philippe. *Les anciens Canadiens*. Montréal: Bibliothèque Québécoise, 1988 [1864].

Clarke, George Elliott. "Must We Burn Haliburton?" *The Haliburton Bi-Centenary Chapbook*. Richard A. Davies, ed. Wolfville, NS: Gaspereau Press, 1997, xx.

——————————— "White Niggers, Black Slaves: Slavery, Race and Class in T.C. Haliburton's *The Clockmaker*." *Nova Scotia Historical Review*. 1994 14:1 13-40.

Callaghan, Morley. *The Loved and the Lost*. Toronto: Stoddart, 1993 [1951].

Frye, Northrop. "Conclusion." *Literary History of Canada*. Second Edition. Volume Two, Carl F. Klinck, ed. Toronto: University of

Toronto Press, 1976 [1965]. 333-364.

Haliburton, Thomas C. *The Clockmaker (First Series)*. Toronto: McClelland and Stewart, 1958 [1836].

Lecker, Robert. "'A Quest for the Peaceable Kingdom': The Narrative in Northrop Frye's Conclusion to the *Literary History of Canada*." *PMLA* 1993 March 108:2 283-93.

Meindl, Dieter. "Canada and American Slavery: The Case of T.C Haliburton." *Slavery in the Americas*. Wolfgang Binder, ed. Wurzburg: Konigshausen & Neumann, 1993, 523-538.

McGregor, Gail. *The Wacousta Syndrome*. Toronto: University of Toronto Press, 1985.

Moodie, Susanna. *Roughing It In the Bush*. Carl Ballstadt, ed. Ottawa: Carleton University Press, 1990 [1852].

Mount, Nick. "In Praise of Talking Dogs: The Study and Teaching of Early Canada's Canonless Canon." *Essays on Canadian Writing*. Spring 1998 No. 63. 76-98.

Morrison, Toni. *Playing in the Dark: Whiteness and the Literary Imagination*. Cambridge: Harvard University Press, 1992.

Richardson, John. *Wacousta*. Douglas Cronk, ed. Ottawa: Carleton University Press, 1987 [1832].

Shadd, Mary. *A Plea For Emigration*. Richard Almonte, ed. Toronto: Mercury Press, 1998 [1852].

Endnotes

1 David Thompson, *Travels in Western America*, Toronto: Macmillan, 1971 [1795].

2 Canadian literature "as antithetical to individuality, masculinity, and social engagement" is my own reading of Frye's Conclusion to the *Literary History of Canada*.

3 Frye's "garrison mentality" is the continuing subject of critical debate. See for instance Gail McGregor and Robert Lecker in Works Cited.

4 For earlier work on Haliburton and Blackness by George Elliott Clarke and Dieter Meindl, see Works Cited.

"Who is she and what is she to you?": Mary Ann Shadd Cary and the (Im)possibility of Black/Canadian Studies

Rinaldo Walcott

A Black feminist historiography would begin with the writings of newspaper editor and publisher Mary Ann Shadd who, as early as 1852, wrote *A Plea for Emigration to Canada West*, a treatise informing Blacks in the United States about the benefits of emigrating to Canada West. She wrote articles on women's rights, and informed her readers through the *Provincial Freeman* newspaper of suffragist meetings in Canada West and the United States. — Bristow et al., 1994

On Sunday, June 7, 1998, *The Toronto Star* published an article with the headline, "Minorities set to be majority." The article relayed that by the year 2000, 54 percent of Toronto's population would be non-white. That same Sunday, *The Toronto Star* report was the lead story on CBC's Sunday Night Report. This information has been occasioning anxiety among those who see themselves as the guardians of Canada's national image: an image minted in one colour — white. But for me, the reports of the coming change in Toronto's population has provoked the opportunity to think about Black people within the coming "super-multicultural" population of Toronto and Canada more generally. For me, this information provides a signal to return to historical contexts; to think about Black migrations; their impact or lack of impact on the national imaginary; as well as who is imagined as a citizen.

I therefore wonder what this new population shift in Toronto — Canada's largest city and most important business centre — will do to the place of racial minorities in national narratives, and more specifically, what it means for Black peoples. To think about this dilemma, I returned to Mary Ann Shadd Cary's *A Plea for Emigration; Or Notes of Canada West*, published in 1852. I wanted to see what conceptions Black people had of Canada and migration prior to the migrations of the 1950s, 60s and 70s, with which Black people are usually associated. I came to one conclusion: we need Mary Ann Shadd Cary, now more than ever.

I turn to Shadd Cary for a number of reasons. Chief among these are: 1) the fact that Shadd Cary occupies a very small place in Canadian Studies and her missing place in feminist studies here (Bristow et al, 1994; Almonte, 1998); 2) her importance to African-American studies, in particular African-American feminist historiography (Ferguson, 1998; Peterson, 1995; Yee, 1992; Rhodes, 1998); and 3) the fact that she eventually left Canada and returned to the US. I believe these three reasons speak in very interesting ways to the place that Black Canadians occupy in the national imaginary.

For this project, I will look at the national imaginary through a discussion of Black/Canadian Studies and the resulting tensions of such a configuration. I am particularly interested in the relationship between Black political cultures in Canada and how those political cultures affect our conceptions of what Canada is. This chapter is a conceptual exercise, concerned with the tensions and contradictions of the interrelatedness of Canadian Studies, Black Studies and Black diaspora discourse. It is an attempt to elaborate a sustainable place in Canadian Studies for Blackness. Mary Ann Shadd Cary will act as our intellectual guide on this elaboration.

In the context of Black Canadian political cultures, figures like Shadd Cary should not only be important as historical models who engaged in struggles for liberation and self-determination, but should also teach us in clearly pedagogical ways how to be a part of a collective Black struggle and still retain an important sense of Black difference. A figure like Shadd Cary should haunt our deliberations on how we envision the future of our nation, and, as Anne McClintock writes, how "nationalism is implicated in gender power" (1995: p.353). Shadd Cary articulated her position on emigration and immigration during a period that was substantively different from our own, and to do so, she had to oppose prominent male abolitionists like Frederick Douglass. I believe her analysis remains relevant for our present circumstances.

I try to think with and, alongside, Shadd Cary as a way to make sense of the space, place and significance of Blackness in Canada, and of the place and space of Canada in the Black diaspora. To do so, I engage with both the limits and the possibilities of Canadian Studies and Black Studies. To announce the impossibility of Black/Canadian Studies is to assert its very possibilities. I assert its possibility in relation to the specificity of the nation, but also, in antagonistic tension with a sensibility that rests beyond national confines — what we might call a diaspora sensibility.

A Brief Biography of Shadd Cary

Mary Ann Shadd Cary was a teacher, mother, journalist, editor, feminist/activist and lawyer. All her identities were related to helping to organize, fashion and refashion the world in which we now live. Shadd Cary arrived in Canada in 1851, one year after the passing of the Fugitive Slave Act of 1850 in the US. The Fugitive Slave Act made it "legally" possible for both freed Black people and fugitives to be reenslaved. Shadd Cary was born in Wilmington, Delaware. She was the oldest of the thirteen children born of Harriet and Abraham Shadd. Both parents were activists who used their home as a station for the Underground Railroad.

Mary Ann Shadd attended a Quaker school and began a teaching career in 1839, which lasted until 1850, teaching in Pennsylvania, New Jersey and New York before moving to Windsor, Canada West. In 1851 she resumed her teaching in Canada, establishing a school for children and their fugitive parents. Shadd Cary believed that the formal education of ex-slaves was one of the most important aspects of liberation, and toward establishing a practice of strong citizenship rights among ex-slaves. Her school, which was partially funded by the American Missionary Association, lasted until about 1853, when the Association withdrew funding. Shadd Cary's school was publicly known as a nonsegregated school, in a time when schools were segregated as a rule. Shadd Cary did not teach again until 1859, then taught until 1863 in Chatham, from where she later returned to the US as the only Black woman to work as a recruiter for the Northern forces during the Civil War.

In 1863 Shadd Cary was appointed Union Army Recruiting Officer to enlist "coloured" soldiers in Indiana. The appointment was made possible through her friend and comrade Martin Delany, an

African American whose voluntary exile was a protest against the Fugitive Slave Act.

While in Canada, Shadd Cary published and edited *The Provincial Freeman*, an abolitionist paper. *The Provincial Freeman* provided Shadd Cary with an organ through which to articulate her political and cultural concerns and to engage in dialogue and argument with her opponents. Shadd Cary published and edited *The Provincial Freeman* from 1854-1855. She was the first Black woman in North America to publish and edit a newspaper.

After the American Civil War, Shadd Cary became the first woman to enter Howard University law school. At age sixty, in 1883, she received her law degree, being one of the first Black women to do so. She died in 1893.

This brief biographical sketch of Shadd Cary's life is merely an attempt to convey some sense of who she was. Shadd Cary, like so many other committed human beings was a figure who stood out in her own time and in historical time. She was one of those unusual human beings who transcended the limitations of human culture as it was lived at her time.

Thinking With and About Shadd Cary

Why does Shadd Cary take me? Why has Shadd Cary been so fascinating to so few scholars? I think that the fascination for Shadd Cary has as much to do with her biography as it has to do with how she stands out as a symbol of a time. But even more pertinent to my concerns are the ways in which her biography, and importantly, her ideas, refuse to be contained by historical time. Shadd Cary's thinking signals for us the limits and excesses of historical time. Her significance is the way that she stands as a figure both in time and across time. This is why we need Shadd Cary now. Her contemporaneity cannot be overlooked.

The cultural and literary critic Homi Bhabha, in trying to demonstrate how the past and the present rely intricately on each other, argues that our returns to the past are always implicated in our thinking about the present. He states that:

Being in the "beyond," then, is to inhabit an intervening space, as any dictionary will tell you. But to dwell "in the beyond" is also, as I have shown, to be part of a revisionary time, a return to the present to redescribe our cultural contemporaneity; to reinscribe our human, historic commonality; *to touch the future on its hither side*. In that sense, then, the intervening space "beyond," becomes a space of intervention in the here and now (1994: p.7).

Shadd Cary as a symbol often appears to be beyond us — outside our reach — only existing as an important "past" figure. This is especially true when we must consider her as an important thinker, and, as African American feminist historian Carla Peterson put it, a "doer of the word." In Shadd Cary's time being a doer of the word meant resisting the gender norms of the period. Such a stance brought with it numerous political pitfalls for Shadd Cary (Rhodes, 1998). But I want to suggest that we can use her as a figure who intervenes in space and time as a signal for how to think about Blackness in Canada. What I am therefore suggesting is that we not only recover Shadd Cary to her place in the historical record (a number of Black feminists historians in Canada are doing that work) but also that we need to think about how her intellectual contributions might inform our contemporary discussions and dialogues. I am suggesting that her ideas are as present now as ever and that her public intellectual role and the consequences she suffered are difficult lessons for thinking Blackness and femaleness together.

Given this, I want to insist on reading Shadd Cary as a figure of the in-between. By this I mean that she sits between Canada and the US; she sits between race and gender; she sits between Canadian Studies and Black Studies; and, for my purposes, she sits between lack and desire. These in-between positions of Shadd Cary are indicative of the sensibilities of Black Canadianness. Blackness in Canada is fashioned by and constituted via the in-between positions, utterances and desires of multiple identifications (Walcott, 1997). These identifications are both locally and nationally constituted and transnationally apparent. Shadd Cary occupied and represents them all. She was a tactician of the in-between.

Carla Peterson, in her discussion of Shadd Cary's work, writes that she "appears to have been impatient with boundaries of all kinds, repeatedly attempting to transcend, if not erase, them" (1995: p.99). Peterson's observations and her assessments of Shadd Cary are clearly borne out in the latter's letters to her various peers (see *The Black Abolitionist Papers*). Peterson writes:

Yet given the attitude of both the dominant culture and the Black male elite toward Black women, Shadd Cary found herself time and again forced to confront boundaries of race, gender, and even nationality. Both her social ideology and her cultural practice came to function, then, as instruments through which she attempted to deconstruct, manipulate, and reconfigure boundaries in order to bring "the desired end" of racial uplift (1995: p.99).

Shadd Cary's position on the limitations of boundaries were very clear. She refused the category of race outright. She preferred to think in terms of "complexional character." Her emigration to Canada was in fact partly motivated by the continuing legal designations of race in the American context and not only by her resistance to the continuation of slavery.

However, Shadd Cary's most enduring and pedagogic insights remain her articulations concerning emigration and the various possibilities for a Black homeland. She participated in and helped to fashion the debate on emigration with her 1852 *A Plea for Emigration*. In one of the many instances of Shadd Cary's challenging of borders, she had her pamphlet printed by a white American printer. This action led to her peer Henry Bibb publicly chiding her. In the pamphlet, Shadd Cary argued for emigration to Canada West as opposed to Haiti and Africa, which were places thought to be more suitable for Black migration at the time. For example, Shadd Cary's critique of the colonization movement, a movement to send Black Americans to an entirely different place was this:

We go further, we want that the colored man should live in America — should "plant his tree" deep in the soil, and whether he turns white, or his neighbors turn black by reason of the residence, is of no moment. He must have his rights — must not be driven to Africa, nor obliged to stay in the States if he desires to be elsewhere. We confess to their views as objectionable, as we know them to be, but this does not close our eyes against the "humbug" connected with this abolition reform, some phases of which would cause a worm-eating New Hollander to hide his head from very disgust (Ferguson, 1998: p.217-218).

She firmly believed in a Black presence in North America and saw North America as "home" for what we might call, in a variation on her term, the complexionally different. Shadd Cary wrote of the climate, the farming, the churches and the various amenities that immigrants would require to successfully resettle. She acknowledged that prejudice existed in Canada West, but suggested that the possibilities for citizenship there were much more open than in the US and the other places (Africa, Haiti, South America, Mexico and some parts of the then British West Indies [Jamaica]) being offered as sites for migration. But upon careful reading of her text, it is clear that Shadd Cary is making an argument for *choice* as opposed to geographic place.

Shadd Cary's position on emigration is what I want to focus on as the place for making her philosophy contemporaneous with present concerns. It seems clear she would have resisted any attempt to imagine a Black presence outside of North America as troubling or problematic.

A House for Blackness: Canadian Studies as "Home"

It can be argued that currently, Blackness in Canadian Studies occupies the place of the repressed. In particular, I am concerned that there is a lack of a sustained theoretical and critical discourse centred on Black Canada within the context of Canadian Studies. Yet Blackness keeps returning to complicate what Canada is and how Canadian Studies aids in the repression of Blackness. The long and now broken silence in St. Armand Quebec, concerning the slave cemetery that was almost ploughed over — called "nigger rock" by locals; the destruction of Africville in Nova Scotia in the sixties; the demolition of Hogan's Alley in Vancouver in the sixties; the changing of the name of Negro Creek Road to Moggie Road in Ontario in 1996 — all are random examples of a wilful attempt to make a Black presence in Canada absent. Attention to these moments or incidents would critically reshape Canadian history and reform Canadian Studies in ways that might cement Blackness within the national imaginary.

Consequently, one might argue that a curious void exists within Canadian Studies. In books and journals that speak to Canadian Studies, individual essays on specific Black texts, or essays on specific Black contexts do speak to and of Blackness in Canada. And yet, there exists a void in Canadian Studies, where Blackness in Canada goes missing. Books and journals setting out to demarcate Canadian Studies make immediately evident the troubling absented presence of Blackness in Canada from the configuration called Canadian Studies. Any survey of major journals in the field demonstrates the limited ways in which Blackness finds itself in Canadian Studies because it is conceived as a recent addition to that field. However, by recovering and thinking with figures like Shadd Cary we can disrupt the falsity of Blackness as merely a recent concern to the nation.

Richard Almonte, editor of the most recent publication of Shadd Cary's *A Plea for Emigration*, poses some crucial questions for Canadian Studies and Shadd Cary's place within it. Almonte argues quite persuasively that Shadd Cary's book belongs to the tradition of "the settlement journal" (1998: p.26). He writes

> In the same year that Shadd published her book in Detroit, another immigrant to Canada, Susanna Moodie, published her settlement journal, *Roughing It in the Bush* (1852), in London, England. Moodie's sister, Catherine Parr Traill, continued this trend two years later with *The Female Emigrant's Guide* (1854), which in later editions was renamed *The Canadian Settler's Guide* (1998: p.26).

Almonte goes on to say, and this is important, that "the importance of the settlement journal or emigrant's guide depends on the audience intended" (1998: p.26). It is not possible to contemplate why Moodie and Parr Traill are canonized in Canadian Studies and Shadd Cary is not. Black people, from the time of Mattieu da Costa and Olivier Le Jeune, have not been an integral part of who we imagine to be Canadian (Winks, 1997; Hill, 1992). To seriously consider Shadd Cary as an instrumental part of the Canadian Studies canon would necessitate a rethinking of how we understand our national formation. It would also place matters of gender, or rather of womanhood, as a central problematic of nation building. In Shadd Cary's case this would require a revision of both the historical and the contemporary understanding of the Canadian nation.

My concern, however, is not solely with absence as the site for correcting a wrong. Instead, I want to read into the void where Black Canadian expressive political cultures might rest. I want to offer a reading that might add to the configuration of Canadian Studies and simultaneously point to why the modern nation, and its corresponding national designations, remain troubling for diasporic Black peoples. It was the inability and the unwillingness of Shadd Cary and many others to live with the vast contradictions of the emerging modern nation of the United States that led to their departure to Canada. It was their desire to find a home where the possibility of living a life of freedom that occasioned many ex-African Americans to also return to the United States after the Civil War.

Therefore, I am arguing for an elaboration of Canadian Studies. Given this position, I believe that the question I need to consider is: can Canadian Studies, as a multi-disciplinary, interdisciplinary and cross-disciplinary configuration and practice, tolerate the repetitive and disruptive return of Blackness? But I also want to enter into dialogue with Canadian Studies to ask other questions. What makes the study of nations special? What do the various policies of nations have to do with how we understand our local, national and transnational identities? What makes us a part of the nation and what causes us to reject the nation? What does Black womanhood do to how we understand the Canadian nation? And what can Canadian Studies not bear to hear in regard to Blackness and the nation? These questions form part of my attempt to unsettle the scene of Canadian Studies, to undermine what we think we mean when we use the term Canadian Studies.

It is my contention that when Blackness works to elaborate Canadianness it simultaneously unsettles Canadianness. That is, Blackness interrupts "Canadian" scenes and simultaneously sets the stage for particular and different enactments of Canadianness. These different enactments of Canadianness are instances of what Homi Bhabha calls "narrating the nation" (1990). Blackness is a counter-narration of the normalized image of Canadian as chromatically white. To consider Shadd Cary in Canadian Studies means that official narrations of the nation must be revised and restaged because Canadian Studies as a configuration is implicated in reproducing particular narratives of the nation — narratives that are often normative notions of the nation as phenotypically white. These narratives simultaneously address Blackness and repress it. Canadian Studies, then, is deeply implicated in many of the "technologies of otherness" (Golding, 1997) that in turn produce Blackness as a recent phenomena in the nation. Of course we now know that the recentness of Blackness is a false construct.

Similarly, to consider gender within the contexts of national formation is to unsettle the nation: when gender is raced, the disruption is massive. When it is a Black woman we must consider, national formation is thrown into chaos. McClintock suggests that a more nuanced and complex theory of nationalism needs to be developed, which can make better sense of the gendering of the nation. Shadd Cary's womanhood, the ways in which her political speech acts were indicted, the ways in which her political acts were circumscribed, and the ways in which she had to both mobilize gender conventions and simultaneously resist those same conventions (Rhodes, 1998) points to the way in which ideologies of gender have historically worked to restrict women's access to the public sphere. When a Black woman is in question, those restrictions are even more severe (Elsa Barkley Brown, 1994), and yet Shadd Cary was able to continue to act within the context of masculinist restrictions.

When Blackness is addressed in Canadian Studies because it is a return, Blackness occupies the place of "the special effect." Blackness is a special effect because conversations concerning Blackness are never sustained — they arise and disappear, only to arise again, as if new. By this, I mean that "Black" work that appears within the context of Canadian Studies is not only disruptive of that configuration, but the work comes to represent and symbolize the benevolence of the configuration — its elasticity — and thus supports one aspect of the nation-state narrative as a place for the special rescue of Blackness: the escape north, to freedom.

"Black" work operates as a special effect because the narrative of the nation never changes, instead it serves to repress how Blackness alters the national narrative of who belongs and how they belong. Indeed, the narrative continues as if nothing happened, only to await yet another return of Blackness. Therefore, despite the great importance of the work, and the contributions and subtractions it makes to narratives of the nation, the work has no sustained force to rethink the terms of Canadian Studies. The configuration of Canadian Studies, like the Canadian nation, can absorb and repress Black interruptions, disruptions and alterations and continue as before. The configuration of Canadian Studies is thus one interesting aspect of the containment of Black Canadianness.

However, I want to turn to the dynamic of repression, and what I would call its mode of address. The dynamic of repression and its silent mode of address constitutes all national narratives to a certain extent. All national narratives require repressions of some sort in their normative narrations. To be more specific, the mutually agreed -upon mode of address of Blackness within Canadian Studies is to be disruptive and to claim the site or space of marginality. Marginality is the place from which Blackness must speak, but is it possible for Blackness to speak from another place? The mode of the address as marginality is not possible without repression, for it is repression that makes marginality possible. That is, the repression of Blackness in Canadian Studies makes possible the mode of the address of marginality through its repeated and repetitive returns: a constant craving for recognition in the face of a continuous erasure.

Every repression has a guaranteed return; but my aim is to attempt to shift the grounds of this continued return. What happens when marginality is not claimed but the centre is assumed instead? Shadd Cary spoke from an assumption of belonging to the centre — she made her citizenship the basis of such an assumption. Her speech acts provoked unsettling moments for both Blackness and whiteness. Shadd Cary threw both race and gender into continual negotiation and negation. I want to fill the void to allow us to use Shadd Cary for an elaboration of Canadianness in order to move away from the continued dynamics of a mode of address of marginality and its continued repression and special effects returns. As a woman and a public intellectual Shadd Cary automatically elaborated the nation in terms of gender and race narratives, these very narratives that must be repressed so that the normative narrative of the nation can take centre stage.

To elaborate Canadian Studies further we would need to curtail the discourse of marginality and denial, and instead suggest a self-assured Black Canadian presence. Shadd Cary is needed now — for she was never not self-assured. I want to suggest that at the moment, Black/Canadian Studies can proceed with little recourse to established or canonical Canadian Studies, but this Black Canadian project, in its self-assuredness, would eventually necessitate a rethinking of Canadian Studies as a whole. Occupying a place "outside," as opposed to a disruptive place "inside," might move us a long way. What I am attempting to do is to highlight one side of diasporic sensibilities, which is the idea of looking beyond.

New Diaspora Times: Canada's Place

Paul Gilroy's *The Black Atlantic* set a new and exciting agenda for Black diaspora studies. Gilroy's work has opened up a discussion concerning transnational Blackness; that is, Blackness as it transmigrates across various regions and nations and accesses a common history of transatlantic slavery and the conditions of a vicious modernism. This transmigration is both literal and metaphorical. Gilroy grounds his work in the nineteenth-century, with readings of W.E.B. Du Bois and Martin Delany, and then reads contemporary cultural practices and engagements from that place (from the Fisk Jubilee Singers to Richard Wright to hip hop artists to Toni Morrison's *Beloved*). *The Black Atlantic* has inaugurated a discussion of Black British and African American cultural and political identifications and cultural sharing. Yet Gilroy's fine study has it weaknesses and lacunae (e.g., Edwards, 1994; Reid-Pharr, 1994).

Particularly striking is his reluctance to seriously consider Black Canada — specifically the back and forth movements across the Canada/US border of the nineteenth-century. This is important in light of the fact that Gilroy spends considerable time analyzing the philosophy of Martin Delany. Delany immigrated to Canada in the 1850s and was a colleague of Shadd Cary. My attempt to think about Mary Ann Shadd Cary is in part a response to some of the Gilroy study's lacunae, and it also differently genders Gilroy's rather masculine genealogy. I am not antagonistic to Gilroy's project; rather, I believe it sets the stage for the questions I wish to ask. I want to suggest, further to Gilroy's *Black Atlantic*, that the complex mixture of Black communities in contemporary Canada offers much for consideration by "new" diasporic discourses. This is especially the case in areas of cultural sharing, borrowing, creolization and governmental "support" of cultural difference — namely, the area of multicultural policies.

Border crossing, in both its metaphorical, literal and historical senses, is important to thinking about the role of "new" diasporic discourses for Black peoples. Border crossings that situate conversations and dialogues at the interstices of Black Studies and Canadian Studies are especially exciting to me. I suggest that both Black Studies and Canadian Studies have woefully neglected Black

Canadian culture. In much of the work of Black Studies where Shadd Cary is referenced, her time in Canada is minimized. Even Peterson's fine reading of Shadd Cary makes use of the trope of the "tourist" to position Shadd Cary as not really Canadian. Worse, in Canadian Studies, Shadd Cary is of little consequence, except among a small number of Black women historians. And, yet, I would argue that both configurations are extremely important in order to map the emergence of a Black diasporic community in Canada — a community whose identifications demonstrate both the possibilities and the limits of nations.

In Jane Rhodes's *Mary Ann Shadd Cary: The Black Press and Protest in the Nineteenth Century*, which attempts to place Shadd Cary in her political and social context, the question of nation and national belonging is paramount. While Rhodes is savvy enough to continually account for Canada as an explicit presence, she nonetheless recreates Shadd Cary as an American citizen. Rhodes does not adequately address how Shadd Cary's politics complicate the category of citizenship. Instead, when Rhodes reports on Shadd Cary taking out Canadian citizenship, she asserts that "In 1865, Mary Ann Shadd Cary was not ready to relinquish her identity as a Canadian. Two months before Lee's surrender at Appomattox, she was issued a Canadian passport..." (1998, p.162). Rhodes goes on to argue that "She falsified her age — in 1865 she would have been forty-two years old — perhaps out of vanity or out of desire to erase the years in Canada that had taken such a toll on her life. But at least for a while, she clung to the quasi-freedom and security that Canada had provided her for almost fifteen years" (1998, p.162).

Rhodes's dismissive comments can provoke a kind of Canadian nationalist defence, which I shall attempt to avoid. However, Rhodes's interpretation of why Shadd Cary lied seems intricately tied to her political committments. First, Rhodes's project is an attempt to reclaim Shadd Cary for a Black American feminist project. Such a reclamation is bounded by national concerns and hence, Shadd Cary must be recouped as an ex-patriot American. To borrow a phrase from Antoinette Burton, Rhodes project demonstrates how "a subject becomes nationalized" (1997, p.238). But what is unresolved in Rhodes's claim, and this is my second point, is that Shadd Cary's solicitation of Canadian citizenship could very well be interpreted as her continuing belief in Canada, not merely as a sanctuary, but as an alternative homeland in North America. Shadd Cary's act of naturalization can therefore much more adequately be interpreted as a political stance full of possibility, as opposed to an attempt to "erase the years in Canada." In this instance Rhodes's project reveals its commitment to reconstituting Shadd Cary too neatly as an US national subject. She might have died in the US, but as a Black woman she always found it deeply inadequate. As Burton points out, drawing on Gilroy, "the notion of deracinated, mobile subjects" is a difficult notion that few have engaged (1997, p.232). I believe Shadd Cary forces us to engage that notion, and yet Rhodes fails to do so.

Our Multicultural Present and Future

I would suggest that what makes the contemporary diasporic community — or communities — in Canada unique and different from both the US and Britain is our policy of official multiculturalism. I take this position in light of some fifteen to twenty years of critiques of Canadian multiculturalism. These critiques have largely cast multiculturalism in two different ways: 1) that it reduces cultures to their basic denominations, which turns them into folklore and 2) that multicultural policies are wasteful government spending that do more to undo the nation than to unite it. Both of these positions rely on each other to make sense and neither accounts for the ways in which the articulation of unofficial multiculturalism as a feature of Canadian society influences and organizes our banal, everyday practices. This will be even clearer when 54 percent of people in Toronto are non-white. Thus the institutional aspects of multiculturalism might require various kinds of retooling, but in the realm of the everyday the assumption of multiculturalism still influences how we live.

In the United States, multiculturalism denotes a variety of positions, very few of which are "official." In Britain, since the demise of the Greater London Councils, in the aftermath of Thatcherism, official multiculturalism is fast disappearing. In Canada, however, federal and provincial multicultural policies have had a tremendous impact on various Black communities.

The policies and discourse of multiculturalism in Canada have allowed for a particular enactment of cultural difference, which in fact pre-empts any coherent or imagined national Black community. This obvious diversity is very different from the US, where a national

Black community sponsors large lobby organizations, such as the NAACP and the Urban League, to promote "national Black interests." In Canada, Black communities proliferate, constituted of continental Africans, Afro-Caribbeans, Black Canadians and others who share certain histories, but who also claim divergent and sometimes antagonistic narratives of the past. Official multicultural policies in Canada bring these differences to the fore in ways that make for a rich understanding of Black Atlantic peoples. These distinctions also affect how different Black communities are incorporated into the nation and what kinds of demands they make of the nation.

However, when we try to think about Canada in the context of larger debates on Black diaspora, limitations become evident. While I am not throwing the concept of diaspora out, I want to engage its current limitations so that we might move beyond them and imbue diasporic discourse with the kinds of conversations that are necessary in the postmodern era, both across and within nations. Shadd Cary as an in-between figure is emblematic of such an approach. Diaspora, as a methodological and conceptual tool for thinking through the relations of Black peoples across and outside national boundaries, is particularly salient in the "new" context of globalization. Shadd Cary was fully aware of what was at stake in making claims within nations and across nations. She not only made demands on the emerging Canadian state, but much of her work was concerned with making demands on the nation south of the border. Shadd Cary exemplifies a diaspora sensibility. She did not leave history behind in her exile status. Instead, she organized, travelled, spoke and eventually edited and published the *Provincial Freeman*, an abolitionist newspaper whose title signals a reference to its place of publication, notwithstanding its concern with aiding in the abolition of US slavery.

If diasporas are possible only because of an original and lengthy dispersal of people that in turn produced a notion of homeland and a possible return — if only imaginative — then other crossings also become central to thinking about theorizing diasporas. The back and forth movements of African Americans and Black Canadians, both in the nineteenth and twentieth centuries, has much to teach us. These migrations make obvious the limitations of current theorizing of the Black diaspora and suggest ways to map its contours more accurately. That is, these migrations demonstrate that for Black North

Americans the permeability of the borders exists not only in relationship to American culture generally, but in relationship to a deeper structure. This idea is exemplified by Shadd Cary's resistance to any wholesale Black emigration outside of North America.

Cultural, social and political questions are of immense importance in the current (re)ordering of Black Studies when this other moment of "rethinking" diaspora is made evident. This point is particularly crucial in assessing Rhodes's contribution, which is largely framed as an address to American scholarship and therefore does not consider how Canada formed Shadd Cary. The fact that Rhodes does not reflect on the place that Canada had in Shadd Cary's biography is telling of the place that Black Canada occupies in some versions of the US Black Studies project. One of the missing links in existing diasporic discourses is that the history and cultural production of Black Canadians has been displaced in conversations and dialogues concerning the Black Atlantic. Thinking concretely about Blackness in Canada, which conceptually and theoretically embraces the tensions and contradictions of diaspora, has much to offer. It would allow us to make sense of what Black Studies can add to the dimensions of thinking about transnational Black cultural practices and identifications. Such thinking would in turn elucidate discourses of home, belonging, nation, Black Studies, Canadian Studies, Black cultural studies and theories of diaspora. In particular, a focus on Black Canadians allows us to highlight nation-state policies like official multiculturalism and the roles those policies play in diasporic identifications and sensibilities. Focussing on crossings and recrossings offers resistance to the seduction of national borders and boundaries; in effect, these crossings can teach us something about how national discourses work. Shadd Cary's life is exemplary of these crossings and Rhodes's study confirms this.

Specifically, the side of diasporic discourses I focus on are the ambivalent, contradictory and discontinuous moments of diasporic experience. Shadd Cary is a good example of the limits of diaspora discourse given her rejection of Haiti as a possible site for the recolonization of Black Americans. Her position speaks to some of the current tensions and contradictions that arise in the context of new forms of imperialism. For example, in an editorial in the *Provincial Freeman* on the various schools of abolitionist thought, Shadd Cary asserted that she reserved the right to refuse the various schools and to simply support the *principle* of abolition since she did not have to play the political game that was necessary in the US. Her conception is important because it sets up a historical prerequisite for how Black Canadians can identify with African-American political positions and simultaneously articulate their own positions. I want to strongly suggest that Shadd Cary spoke and acted from political conviction, desire and commitment — not from nationalistic yearning or desire.

How do we maintain a discussion of crucial Black differences in the context of increasing pressures to discuss Black diasporic connectedness?

Conclusion: A House Redesigned?

We need Mary Ann Shadd Cary now more than ever. As the nation continues to figure out its various possibilities, Black Canadians might use Shadd Cary's insights and creative insubordinations to articulate our multiple and conflicting relations to this nation. Shadd Cary not only refused the category of nation but she rejected gender codes when they did not work to her advantage; and she identified with the oppressed out of political connections, not biological realities.

The contemporary proliferation of Black Canadian literature, film, art, music and theatre requires that we think along with Shadd Cary concerning questions of community. Shadd Cary's irreverent questioning of community was for her the basis for making it better and for making it work. Her public disputes with prominent Black abolitionists can be understood as her attempt to forge alliances based upon common political strategies and goals and not solely on the question of race.

Furthermore, Shadd Cary can help us not only refashion how we understand Blackness in Canada but also to redesign the very house that is the nation. My return to Shadd Cary is in part a need to invent a Black Canadian discourse that reflects the continuous and discontinuous moments of Black Canadian life. This discourse can in turn produce a grammar that locates Blackness in a history that is longer than simply the latest migrations (see Walcott, 1997: p.133-149).

Sylvia Sweeney recently made a film entitled *Breaking the Ice: The Mary Ann Shadd Story* (1997). *Breaking the Ice* takes it title from Shadd Cary's August 1855 "Adieu" article as editor of the *Provincial*

Freeman, where she declared that

> colored women, we have a word — we have "broken the
> Editorial ice," whether willing or not, for your class in America;
> so go to Editing, as many of you as are willing, and able, and as
> soon as you may, if you think you are ready (Bearden and
> Butler, 1977: p.163).

In that year Shadd had effectively been forced out of the paper she
had founded because of public outrage when it was discovered that
M.S .Shadd (her editorial name) was a woman (Bearden and Butler,
1977; Almonte, 1998; Rhodes, 1998). It is with this radicality in
mind that Shadd Cary's life has much to teach us. Her ideas on what
is required to make our citizenship a home of possibilities should be
our first lesson. We need Shadd Cary now, in this moment of
globalization, in this moment of reimagining who and what a
Canadian might be.

Works Cited

Almonte, R. "Introduction." A *Plea for Emigration*; *Or Notes of
Canada West*. Toronto: Mercury Press, 1998.

Bearden, J. Butler, J. *The Life and Times of Mary Shadd Cary*. Toronto:
NC Press Ltd, 1977.

Bhabha, H. "Introduction: narrating the nation"; and
"DissemiNation: time, narrative, and the margins of the modern
nation" *Nation and Narration*, H. Bhabha (ed.). New York: Routledge,
1990.

—. "Introduction: Locations of Culture." *The Location of Culture*.
London: Routledge, 1994.

Bristow, P. [coordinator], Brand, D., Carty, L., Cooper, A.P.,
Hamilton, S., Shadd, A. *We're Rooted Here and They Can't Pull Us
Up: Essays in African Canadian Women's History*. Toronto: University
of Toronto Press, 1994.

Brown, E.B. "Negotiating and Transforming the Public Sphere:
African American Political Life in the Transition from Slavery to
Freedom." *Public Culture*, Vol.7, No.1, Fall 1994: 107-146.

Burton, A. "Who Needs the Nation? Interrogating 'British' History".

Journal of Historical Sociology, Vol.10, No.3, September 1997: 227-248.

Edwards, N. "Roots, and Some Routes not Taken: A Caribcentric Approach to *The Black Atlantic*." *Found Object*, Issue 4, Fall 1994: 27-35.

Ferguson, M., ed.. *Nine Black Women: An Anthology of Nineteenth-Century Writers from the United States, Canada, Bermuda, and the Caribbean*. New York: Routledge, 1998.

Gilroy, P. *The Black Atlantic: Modernity and Double Consciousness*. Cambridge: Harvard University Press, 1993.

Golding, S. ed. *The Eight Technologies of Otherness*. London: Routledge, 1997.

Hill, D.G. *The Freedom-Seekers: Blacks in Early Canada*. Toronto: Stoddart [The Book Society of Canada Limited], 1992 [1981].

McClintock, A. *Imperial Leather: Race, Gender and Sexuality in the Colonial Contexts*. New York: Routledge, 1995.

Peterson, C. *"Doers of the Word": African American Women Speakers and Writers in the North (1830-1880)*. New York: Oxford University Press, 1995.

Reid-Pharr, R. "Engendering the Black Atlantic." *Found Object*, Issue 4, Fall, 1994: 11-16.

Rhodes, J. *Mary Ann Shadd Cary: The Black Press and Protest in the Nineteenth Century*. Bloomington: Indiana University Press, 1998.

Ripley, C. P., ed. *The Black Abolitionist Papers: Volume II Canada, 1830-1865*. Chapel Hill: The University of North Carolina Press, 1986.

Shadd, M.A. *A Plea for Emigration; Or Notes of Canada West*. Toronto: Mercury Press, 1998 [1852].

Walcott, R. *Black Like Who?: Writing Black Canada*. Toronto: Insomniac Press, 1997.

Winks, R. *The Blacks in Canada*. Montreal&Kingston: McGill-Queens University Press [Yale University Press], 1997 [1971].

Yee, S.J. *Black Women Abolitionists: A Study in Activism, 1828-1860*. Knoxville: The University of Tennessee Press, 1992.

My Dearest Child

Joy Mannette

My dearest child,

How shall I tell the story of who you are? You are an African Canadian man-child. It is easy to speak of the "African" and of the "Canadian" but neither naming captures who you are. Indeed, you problematize the notion of "Canadian." Yet, in your little brown body and in your naming, Rakgwedi Manet Ramphore, you express something about the story of Canada. You are a Canadian citizen but you carry your own passport.

Who are you *puna* and what is your story? *Ra, man; kgwedi, moon — a state of being, not a noun.* You are named by *Nkono* as the ancestors proclaimed: "A boy child will take the name of the first Rakgwedi who was a pastoralist. You carry a strong spirit, *puna*; never forget that."

"What a beautiful name!" exclaims a skater at Toronto's Nathan Phillips Square, a man who embodies the Canadian ideal: tall, strong, fair-haired, blue-eyed and a good skater. More frequently the response is, "what a mouthful;" and "how do you say that." You let people call you "Rock" because you want to belong and don't understand what it means to be denied your name. You are only eight years old. You know you are "brown" and somehow "African" and you know that Mamma is "white" — well, sort of pinkish, actually. You sing "Oh, Canada" and "Nkosi sike'lele" but Pokémon is often more important. In grade three you are asked to do a unit on pioneers. You know, it's like Toronto's Black Creek Pioneer Village. You went on a trip there once with your daycare. What's this notion of "pioneer" got to do with more recent settlers of Canada? It's too prosperous, too land-bound, too ethnically exclusive, too "way back then." *Ntate* is a settler; Mamma is too; but "pioneer" has nothing to do with the way history lives in them and, so, in you.

In naming you Manet, Mamma reclaimed her patrilineal name from its nineteenth-century anglicization. You are Acadian, *puna*. Your *patrimoine*, through me, your mother, finds its place in a small village, Chezzetcook, on the eastern shore of Nova Scotia. About forty-five kilometres north of Halifax, this place of tides was a haven of Catholicism in a sea of Protestantism. It was French but only in the 1980s was it honoured by being named "acadien" by the Centre for Acadian Studies and the University of Moncton. Besides, Acadian, there are Romas and Murphys, along with Mannettes, Bellefontaines, LaPierres, Fouches, and Bonnevies. When I was a child, before Vatican II, a French homily and French hymns were sung in the epicentre of the *parroise*; but also on Christmas there was "mumming," when we disguised ourselves and roamed door to door, giggling and excited not to be uncovered.

But did I tell you too, *puna*, that we children also learned to call the Christmas treat of Brazil nuts, "nigger toes," and that we sorted our playmates with "eenie, meenie, mini, mo; catch a nigger by the toe?" Perhaps this explains why, in your words, Mamma "went on and on" at your Toronto daycare, when she found you and your playmates using "eenie, meenie, mini, mo; catch a tiger by the toe."

After midnight mass at a Chezzetcook Christmas, we used to go to my grandparent's home and eat paté — rabbit, salt pork and onions, cooked in bread dough and basted with drippings. Our land, the Mannette land, like that of our neighbours stretched from the Atlantic inlet to Porter's Lake — an anglo incursion — which the busy Acadian men dyked so that the sea would not come in. What was it about these Acadians and their dykes; their struggle against the sea both for land and on little boats? What was this attachment to the land; the peasant's dream of what was not possible across the water; the deep and sustaining bond with earth and water; and learning to tell the time by the moon, the plants and the tides? The little boats were curiously flat-bottomed and had room for only one man and one boy, so as to be able to navigate the estuaries at both low and high tides. We were the only known Acadians who ate sauerkraut, learned from our German neighbours. It is said that the cattle grazed on the saltmarshes. Your genealogy is too complicated, said the Acadian genealogist; not "laine pure," as the Quebecois would have it, nor the Chezzetcook variation — "cocques pures," perhaps.

The Mannette men were long livers. I remember my great-grandfather, Grandad Fred, ne Frédéric. He died in 1961 at age ninety-seven when I was nine years old. The nuns at the village school said, "Why should she go to the funeral; he was only her great-grandfather." I must have persisted because I remember following the coffin into the church and watching its descent into the damp ground in St. Anselm's graveyard, the only place where I now can find our name. You are the last of the Mannette bloodline, *puna*. Will you go back to the earth in that graveyard as Mannettes always have? Will you have to choose between the fog and damp of Chezzetcook, and the dust and calabash-red soil of Mohlakeng, the place of reeds, in South Africa? It is in Mohlakeng where lies *ntatemaholo*, your Sotho grandfather for whom I taught you the rituals of soil and calling on the ancestors when you were but three years old.

My Acadian great-grandfather stood tall and spare and carried a walking stick to shoo away troublesome snakes. He shared his gossip with me. I found him kind but my anglo grandmother, Hannah, said he was a hard man who sent his son, my grandfather, called "crooked Willie," out to work when he was seven years old. My anglo grandmother was full of aspirations for upward mobility and stories from her "black sheep" father, a charming and handsome alcoholic wife beater who sprang from minor gentry. His father was a magistrate. "Remember girl," he told Nanny, "there's lords and ladies in your family." Nanny, lonely and isolated, kept me apart from the Acadian neighbours and decried her husband's insufficient table manners. She rigorously instilled in Mamma a sense of being different and better than the Chezzetcook people. Is that why her daughters married anglo-Celtic men and welcomed their new naming, Spencer and Bell? As a university professor, Nanny would have believed I was following her lessons. As a young girl, *puna*, Mamma did, at the nunnish Mount Saint Vincent Academy. There I cohabited with the daughters of the Halifax Catholic elites. I came to despise where I came from and my nascent Acadian accent was shamed out of me. Yet, as a scholar, the more I moved "up," the more I was drawn back.

Crooked Willie was my grandfather, your great-grandfather, *puna*, whose mother, Marie Charlotte, had died giving life to a misshapen boy-child. The women, Mannette-by-marriage, losing their names and, thus, the sense of "mix," married and died young, usually in childbirth, after bearing about twelve children each, only half of whom survived infancy. There were the Mannette women, all named Marie — Honore, Celestine, Berthe — the men, all named Josephe — Etienne, Guillaume, Georges, Luc. Josephe William, my "Grampy," born in 1895, "the year of the white mice," he said; the year of the raising of the current Ste. Anselm's, whose architecture signals its communal significance. It is made of clay brick from the Chezzetcook mudflats, which also made its way to the fine homes and businesses of the building boom of 1870s downtown Halifax, following a fire which wiped out nearly all the clapboard edifices. My Grampy could turn his hand to anything but he could not read much more than the church bulletin and newspaper headlines — and that only much later when he taught himself in his seventites.

They were skilled, the Chezzetcook men, and they "went to market," exchanging animals, produce, and legendary Chezzetcook clams for the edification of the townspeople. Loading the ox-pulled wagon in the middle of the night, they travelled the rutted road to catch the first ferry from Dartmouth across the harbour to the Halifax City Market, where cousin Reggie Mannette's family now bring seasonal transplants from their greenhouses which go on to the pots and small green spaces of the city. And the children picked berries and flowers, mayflowers and blueberries, bringing on corrosive competition with our neighbours, the "coloured people" of Preston: "Never buy blueberries from coloured people, they pee on them first" was my first remembered association of "Black" with dirty.

You were born in Nova Scotia, *puna*; does that make you a Black Nova Scotian? Black Nova Scotians are not as long-standing as the Acadians, whose first church-recorded presence in Chezzetcook predates the Black Nova Scotian Preston settlement by at least thirty years. Black Loyalists, as they are now known, were named as a group largely through the efforts of Sylvia Hamilton, who in 1983, on the bicentennial of the coming of the Loyalists to Nova Scotia, insisted that Black people were also part of that crucial migration from the fallen New England colonies. The Black Loyalists were free men and women "of colour," former slaves, to whom British commanders in the field had promised freedom of person and free land and provisions to any who would abandon their slave masters and cross behind the British lines to fight for the British cause. Three thousand Black Nova Scotians — soldiers, pilots, reconnaisance men, wheelwrights, smiths, farmers, seamstresses, cooks, washerwomen — formed part of skilled immigrants to the colony. One third of the initial Loyalist migration the British loaded on ships, after the fall of New York in 1781, and brought to Nova Scotia. Black, free men and women built the towns and cleared the farms, changing forever Nova Scotia from British possession to colony and establishing the character of what, one hundred years later, became Canada.

Other Black people — the Jamaican Maroons, for example — went on to construct the Halifax Citadel and, held in high esteem by colonial authorities for their military prowess, were mustered into a regiment, in anticipation of Napoleonic incursions. The British were never able to militarily defeat the Maroons; rather, British commanders tricked them into a peace settlement and then forced them to relocate. However, the Maroons successfully agitated for removal from Nova Scotia, and in 1799 they were sent to Sierra Leone to put down the insurrection against the British of other Black Nova Scotians there. But I am getting ahead of myself, *puna*.

Settled on the poorest land, impossible even for subsistence farming, outside the boundaries of the white towns, the Black Loyalists found precarious freedom in the slave society Emancipation came only two generations later, with the 1834 Act of Emancipation of the British Parliament. American raiders routinely sailed under sanguine British eyes into the coastal communities, reclaiming human property for their Republican masters. Black Nova Scotians were rendered a permanent but marginalized working class and refused entry to places of worship as well as schools. If permitted in Anglican churches — the state religion — Black Nova Scotians were consigned to the "slave galleries." One of these remains in Halifax's St. Paul's Church, built in 1749, where, ironically, the imperial eagle shapes the pulpit and regimental banners laud the imperial triumphs, including the 1899 Boer War. The last Black/white racially segregated school closed in Nova Scotia in 1956, four years after Mamma was born, *puna*. Not to mention the Indian Residential School at Schubenacadie which was not closed until the 1970s. Elsewhere, Black Nova Scotians were even legally denied basic public entertainment as the largest Loyalist town of Rosetown banned "Negro frolics" in 1785.

Among the Black Nova Scotians came literate and worldly men — including several preachers, and the enterprising "Thomas Peters man" of Annapolis Royal. In the late 1780s, Thomas Peters worked his passage to London, where, together with the emancipationists at work for the Black Poor of that city, he petitioned the Crown for the fair enforcement of the proclamation that British commanders had made in the field during the Revolutionary War. They argued that freedom of person was meaningless without the means to sustain free life. The British promptly sent out to Halifax John Clarkson of the Society for the Propagation of the Gospel to organize the Sierra Leone relocation. Colonial authorities thwarted Clarkson at every turn, as landowners, alarmed at the potential loss of cheap Black labour, stymied Clarkson's efforts. But in January, 1791, two ships loaded with twelve hundred Black Nova Scotians embarked for Sierra Leone; for the "best and brightest" of the Black Nova Scotians, this signified leaving behind the unfulfilled promises of the "promised land," Nova Scotia; and looked ahead to their new dream: back to Africa.

They left behind decimated Black Nova Scotian communities, soon to be replenished with another empty imperial promise, during the War of 1812. For the Crown, Clarkson's Sierra Leone relocation was an expedient resolution of two colonial problems: to quell dissent in Nova Scotia, and to establish a British-allied Black commercial and military presence in West Africa. Today, in war-ravaged Sierra Leone, the Creoles of the Black Nova Scotian exodus are still distinguished from the Mende and other groups, in terms of language, custom and status.

Among those who sailed for Sierra Leone was Lydia Jackson. In the words of George Elliott Clarke, Black Nova Scotian poet, Lydia Jackson was "Black as stars, slaved and served, slaved and starved; in this rough land, cold and hard, water and rock were her guard." In Nova Scotia Lydia Jackson, "slave madonna," was owned by Dr. Buhlman. You can still see his fine town house in Lunenburg, *puna*, marked by a plaque, an important feature of this "Dutch" tourist site's walking tour. Lydia Jackson, unlettered Black Loyalist, had been abandoned by her husband upon arrival in Guysborough, and was then tricked into signing a thirty-nine-year Bill of Indenture, which was then sold to the good Lunenburg doctor. "And when she came to him, with the news [Buhlman's rapes had born fruit], he knew just what to do; he beat her; he beat her 'til she was black and blue and the poor child, he died when due." Hearing of Clarkson's relocation scheme, Lydia Jackson traveled overland some 150 kilometres to Halifax, presented herself to Clarkson and sought passage. Clarkson arranged for her court appearance, where the chicanery of the indenture was revealed and Lydia Jackson was declared a free woman. She also overrode Clarkson's admonition that all women who embarked on the voyage to Sierra Leone must have a man to assume responsibility for them.

Recorded in the Ste. Anselme parish register, 1761, the year of the Royal Proclamation, our first ancestor in Chezzetcook, one Georges Mannette; it is said that he and his brother made their way to Chezzetcook from fallen Louisbourg on Ile Royale and that they had been soldiers. Along the way, Georges had acquired a Portuguese wife, Charlotte, probably at the important fishing station, Ship Harbour in Guysborough, while more Mannettes, likely Georges' brothers, established themselves at nearby Larry's River. Chezzetcook and Larry's River were the only two Mannette root places known to Mamma, until just last year when I was told by a Trinidadian acquaintance that her cousin had married a Mannette — with the same anglicization of the name. Only two months ago, *puna*, Mamma came across a website which informed her that Ellie Mannette, also of Trinidad, is honoured as the twentieth century "father of the steel pan." These are more strands in the weave of who you are, *puna*. Another theory is that Chezzetcook was settled by returning Acadians who had hidden in the woods during the 1755 Grand Derangement.

Black people continued to go to and from Nova Scotia. Eighteen twenty one brought the Black Refugees. It also marked the departure of "100 Negroes" for Trinidad. Back and forth between Nova Scotia and New England, Black Nova Scotians carved routes that confound accepted national boundaries of the master narrative of North American history. In the burgeoning industrial centres of the northern United States, Black Nova Scotians sought the dignity and opportunities denied to them in Nova Scotia. The 1890s brought "mechanics" from the Caribbean to Halifax industries and the nationally vital coal and steel production of Cape Breton. In 1918, one third of Canada's wealth was generated in Cape Breton coal and steel. Yet today, in Sydney's Whitney Pier — an ethnic enclave separated from Sydney proper by the steel plant — the Barbados flag flies proudly over the churchyard of the African Methodist Church on Hankard Street during the "Caribbean Picnic."

Organized into a racially segmented labour force at "the plant" and in "the pit," Black men were denied union membership during the great labour struggles of the 1910s and 1920s. Only much later, in the 1970s, Winston Ruck emerged as a union leader. Black women ran boarding houses and served hot dinners to plant workers from their homes, "conveniently" located next to the coke ovens. The racial hierarchy ensured that the closer to the plant you lived, the lower was your status. But in 1937, the famed champion of the back to Africa movement, Marcus Garvey, spoke to an impressive crowd in Whitney Pier.

Throughout Black Nova Scotia, in the late nineteenth and early twentieth centuries, Black women toiled "in service" and as "Saturday girls." "A dollar a day for back-breaking, sweat-soaked" labour, writes Nova Scotian poet Maxine Tynes. "Helen was somebody's 'girl,' some white lady's 'girl,' this never-married Black woman… What did my little girl mind know?…the secret whispers of lady talk…She died 'in service.'" On through the twentieth century, Black people continued to arrive to Nova Scotia as nurses, lawyers, physicians, teachers, from the Caribbean and Africa. Then, in the 1970s and 80s came the "international students," like your father, *puna*, slapped with higher fees — a particularly onerous burden against "Third World" currencies. And the sleeping car porters followed the rails to Montreal, Winnipeg and northern American cities; sleeping car porter, the career ceiling for Black Nova Scotian men until the 1960s. Sometimes, the porters married into Black communities on their "routes;" sometimes they brought their wives "home," home to Africville.

Africville was destroyed by Halifax urban planners in the spirit of 1960s urban renewal. Ironically, *puna*, Mamma's 1967 Mount Saint Vincent Academy yearbook features a photo of "Mount girls" against the backdrop of a bulldozed Africville and the half-completed "new" bridge, the A. Murray McKay. Wedged between the city dump, the railway line and the prison, Africville was home to so many sleeping car porters. "Where the road ended, Africville began," stated the narrator of the NFB's *Remember Africville*. But Africville lives today in the Africville Genealogical Society; and at the annual August picnic at Seaview Park, which now marks that fallen Black space. People come from all over Canada and the US, come "home to Africville." As

George Elliot Clarke put it, "Nova Scotia is such a hard place to stay."

Nineteen sixty eight saw the coming of the Black Panthers and the pinnacle of "Rocky's revolution." But that year also marks the denial of burial to a Black child in a white cemetery at St. Croix, Nova Scotia. Before Rosa Parks said "No" to the back of the bus, in 1947 New Glasgow, Mrs. Desmond, a Halifax beautician," refused to sit in the "coloured" balcony of that city's cinema. No disrespect to Miss Rosa Parks but Mrs. Desmond said "no" too. Why, then, does the history of Black American resistance eclipse what Black people in Nova Scotia did, in the spirit of resistance, throughout the long history of their settler presence in Nova Scotia. In 1968, the Black Panthers in fact inspired panic and quick containment from the provincial fathers, in the form of the Nova Scotia Human Rights Commission; and in 1970, provincial funding was established for the Black United Front. Rocky Jones, then in his fifties, called to the Nova Scotia Bar, came home to Nova Scotia fresh from SNCC to work with youth in the Halifax city projects and help direct the fate of the people of Africville and of those moving from rural areas. Afroed, bearded, dashiki-ed, "Black and Proud," Rocky Jones scared the hell out of white folks who feared that "The chickens had come home to roost" in Nova Scotia. Predictably, people ignored Joan Jones, whom Mamma thinks is actually more "scary" to white privilege, *puna*.

The 1970s and 80s brought the rise of what Mamma calls the "Black Renaissance," an explosion of music, writing, art and community consciousness. It is the "little children [who] lead them." The Cultural Awareness Youth Groups (CAYG) were brought to life by young Trinidad-born David Woods, who had come to Nova Scotia at the age of twelve. Banned in some Metro Halifax schools — and where permitted relegated to "extra-curricular" status — the CAYG spawned *Four the Moment*, Delvina Bernard's a capella group. " Three Black and one white women — an appropriate balance, " they modelled themselves on the American *Sweet Honey in the Rock*, and sang Langston Hughes's "Nothing Lights a Fire Like a Dream Deferred." "History singing," claimed Delvina when *Four the Moment* put to song the powerful poetics of George Elliott Clarke. Did you know, *puna*, that it was George Elliott Clarke who renamed Black Nova Scotians "Africadians?" A shock to Mamma's *Acadienne* sensibilities, it was still a powerful claim to place. *Four the Moment*, which went on to be a darling of the Canadian "definer" Peter Gzowski, made their debut at a 1981 "Smash the Klan" rally in downtown Halifax.

The KKK, *puna*, had a presence in rural Nova Scotia that dated back to the 1930s. It was the CAYG at Cole Harbour High School that fine-tuned Delvina Bernard's early race consciousness. Cole Harbour High School has gone on to Canadian notoriety as the site of late 1970s and early 1980s race struggles (named "race riots" by alarmist media). Did Mamma tell you, *puna*, that I taught there and coached the girls' basketball team from 1979 to 1981? Did I tell you that I "took a punch" during a racially charged fracas at a school dance there in 1980? Did I tell you, *puna*, that I quit teaching in 1981 because I could no longer be an enforcer of systemic racism in that school, and that is why my MA thesis and Ph.D. dissertation are on Black Nova Scotians?[1] In "Lullaby for Cole Harbour", *Four the Moment*, sing "How can they stop the tears about to fall, knowing that another child's innocence is lost? And how can they start to teach African ways, when buses are driving the children away?"

Black Nova Scotian communities continue to lose their future as the young venture forth to Montreal, Calgary, and Toronto. In search of the "promised land," they all too often become statistics of drugs and guns and men's violence. "I only know that it's a crime to take a life and lose your own," laments *Four the Moment*. And still, the young persist in staking the audacious claim to be Nova Scotian, and, thus, Canadian. This is an important point, *puna*. The way regional identity works is that you are Nova Scotian first and Canadian second. However, I have found, *puna*, that people in Toronto just don't get it. Furthermore, it is only central Canadians of a certain class or ethnic background who go around trying to define "Canadian identity;" the rest of us know who we are because we are rooted in a place and a time. That's part of the reason why the master narrative of Canadian history is so skewed and incomplete, *puna*: you've got all these academics of a certain class, ethnicity, and gender telling us the story of who we are. However, it's only the story of who they are, or who they want to be.

"You don't have to play the bagpipes to be Nova Scotian," asserts Sylvia Hamilton's searing NFB documentary *Speak It!* And Winston's girl, graduating university student Marlene Ruck, matter-of-factly stated at the 1989 Atlantic Association of Sociologists and

Anthropologists Meeting that "we are strangers in our homeland...which sings of the contributions of the Celtic peoples." Stellar contributions to the British Crown and Canada have never conferred the rights and privileges of citizenship on Black Nova Scotians. The long lines of Black Loyalists, miners and steelworkers, "girls" and charladies; the World War I Black Battalion; the first "Canadian" recipient of the British Victoria Cross — Thomas Hall for valour in the Crimea; the Order of Canada for William P. Oliver; the Harry Jerome Award for Clothilda Yackumchuck; and other community service efforts, attest to this.

The weave of who you are becomes more differentiated in the late 1980s. Mamma was then working at the University College of Cape Breton and was involved in pro-bono work during the Mi'kmaq Treaty Trials, which established that the *1752 Treaty* "of peace and friendship" between the British Crown and the Mi'kmaq Nation, had not been extinguished. Mamma's mother's people came from Cape Breton, *puna*, more displaced people, the Parkers, the Kennedys, and the MacNeils, of the Scottish highland clearances and the Irish potato famine. Mamma's mother, on hearing about my appointment, was happy I was "going home;" I knew better.

It's ironic, though, *puna*, that as I edit this writing, I am watching on television the funeral of forty-year-old John Morris Rankin. He was not only a brilliant musician, but a good man. Mamma remembers John Morris as a just a "little fella," whose legs were too short for him to reach the pedals of the piano in the parlour of Uncle Dan's and Aunt Mary's farm house in Brook Village, Inverness County, Cape Breton, Nova Scotia. I can see and hear him still, along with the late, great fiddler, Dan R. MacDonald, his big stomach straining his white shirt. The music was magic, *puna*. You just had to dance. As my dear friend Elizabeth Beaton said of the mourning for the loss of John Morris, "Cape Bretoners still know how to pick their heroes." John Morris Rankin was a Canadian hero, *puna*. When I was a little girl, my family would travel by car each summer from Elliot Lake, Ontario, where my father worked in the uranium mines. First we would go to Boston and visit there with my mother's transplanted Cape Breton kin. For all of us, though, the best part of the holiday was going to Brook Village. It was on that farm that Mamma learned about taking the cows to pasture and feeding the chickens. Everybody worked on the farm. We always made it to Brook Village to make hay.

The work teams of men went from field to field, farm to farm, and laboured from the time the morning milking was done till it was dark to get the hay in before the rain. I remember, too, *puna*, that after the supper dishes were done and the cows were taken to their night pasture, eveybody would get cleaned up and dressed up and go to a "ceildh" or dance — one for every night of the week, except Sundays at the Inverness County village halls. The Rankins were related in some way, I never knew just how, which is why I came to see and hear little John Morris.

However, my coming to Cape Breton in 1987 was in a different time and space. Also, when news of my relationship with your African father made the rounds, one of my students was quizzed in a Cape Breton job interview on how I could "lower myself" in that way. Nurses in the maternity ward of your birth gave pause once they saw your father. Strangers would exclaim in surprise, when they saw the baby (you) with me, "He's so beautiful!" I knew what they had expected. Actually, it was among Mi'kmaw people on the Eskasoni First Nation in Cape Breton that Mamma came to feel most at home. It was Eleanor Johnson who told me that "All you can really do is love them," as I agonized about the racism you would encounter, *puna*. I knew that Nova Scotia was no place to bring up a "Black" child. It's the "one drop rule," *puna*. Eleanor Johnson, who so despised the academic "cognitive tourists" who told stories about the Mi'kmaq, taught me so very much about how to teach Mi'kmaw people the book knowledge of the university. It was Marie Battiste, the first Mikmaw with a Ph.D., who organized a "party" for this *aglasiew* who knew so little about babies and how best to take care of them. For the Mi'kmaw, to celebrate a baby's birth before the fact was a strange white custom; so they organized a party. The men, including *ntate*, were shooed outside with the beer and the barbecue, and thirty or so Mi'kmaw women provided tea and food and talk, and wonderful baby stuff for you, *puna*. There was much punning and laughter, healing loving laughter, and you kicked vigorously. I think you liked it too. I was overwhelmed, and it wasn't just "hormones" that brought me to tears. Many of these Mi'kmaw women who had so little in material goods had bought you such lovely things and shared their baby wisdom with me through "telling-story," as Marie Battiste names it.

During the Treaty Trials, Sakeg Henderson had organized a group of us, Mi'kmaw and non-native, and we pored over the documents of the British Colonial Office, consulted with Elders, strategized with the lawyers, and attended court, unless we were teaching. It was these documents, the much-reviled record of imperial interest, that were touted in the court by an academic historian, University of New Brunswick's Steven Patterson, as the "truth" of the treaty process. I wrote and delivered a stinging indictment of Patterson's historiography and the questionable ethics of his paid secondment to the Crown Attorney. In my *Making of the Expert Witness*, Mamma was shunned as "ungentlemanly" by other academics because I had not alerted Patterson to my work and invited him to debate! But, that, *puna*, is another story.

One of these documents revealed to me the 1754 translation efforts of a certain Jean Baptiste, a Mi'kmaq "Roman" convert, from a fishing community, "some leagues north of Halifax." Well, I knew that the only Catholic fishing community "some leagues north of Halifax" was Chezzetcook! When I consulted the genealogy of the first Acadian families of Chezzetcook, prepared by St. Anslem's Monsignor Melanson in the mid-twentieth century, I found that Jean Baptiste was our ancestor, the father of Grampy's mother; we had always talked about Grandfather Murphy's and usually went there in August to pick blueberries. Monsignor's Melanson's labours also recorded that the first Catholic place of worship in Chezzetcook was known as the Mi'kmaq Chapel. Now, the Mi'kmaq Nation had been a Catholic nation since 1610, when Sagamow Membertou embraced Catholicism. Material history from the Nova Scotia Museum had also told us that the harbours of Nova Scotia's Eastern Shore were important summer and fall camping sites for the Mi'kmaq before they wintered inland, near Schubenacadie. There was much communal interdependence and friendship between the Mi'kmaq and the Acadians, bound as they both were in French allegiance, faith, and struggle against the English. There was much intermarriage as well. Of course there was Mi'kmaq blood among the first Acadian families of Chezzetcook! All I had to do was look in the mirror to recognize the "skinny-faced" Mi'kmaq prototype, with high cheek bones and prominent nose; the face of my Grampy; the face of his daughter, Adah, who believed herself unattractive so much of her life, in comparison with her round-faced, short-nosed sister. However, before I could recognize this in myself, I had to "see" this as a possibility. So, the weave of who you are is rich in skeins, *puna*.

What about *ntate, puna?* Sydney James Ramonametsi Ramphore — freedom fighter for Azania — Sotho and Tswana but taking his lineage in patriarchy from his father's Sotho line. Born into apartheid South Africa and carrying his English names, his parents sought to keep him safe from the 1970s student struggles, sending him to be educated by Irish monks in a Free State boarding school. They expected, as did Sydney, that education would be better there than Mohlakeng Township schooling. It was not. Your father says, "*thato ke lesedi*," education is light. And the light was fire, burning the schools, making the country ungovernable. The schools and their education for inferiority are where your father learned to be an expert gardener. At the 1976 Student Uprising (again, "the little children shall lead them") your father took a bullet and kept running: to stop is to die. Your father learned to be a cadre in APLA, took part in covert operations within the country to the sound of an oft-sung freedom song, "*Ntate, bana bashwa, Father, your children are dying.*" APLA was the armed wing of the Pan Africanist Congress, the infamous PAC whose motto was "One settler, one bullet." There is something to be learned there, *puna*, about pioneers.

The young man who took a bullet and kept running became a man. On the run, he crossed the Limpopo, hearing the crocodiles take cadres in silence: anything to thwart the Groot Crocodile.[2] In the camps, safe houses and prisons of front-line states, *ntate* finds the political organizations as deadly as the Boer. In the former Yugoslavia, he fine-tunes espionage. In Libya, he shows the mettle of *Afrique du Sud.* He joins cultural groups touring other African countries and Europe in order to gain support for the struggle. He was part of the PAC delegation to the United Nations in New York. This is your father, *ntate*, who speaks nine languages but not "standard" English, as he soon learned in a Canadian university. To stop is to die.

Ntate came to Canada as a political refugee. He said, "among the nations of the West, Canada had such a good reputation in its support of the struggle." *Ntate* came to get book knowledge and to find in Canada what is impossible in South Africa — a university degree. In his eighteen years in exile, *ntate* was determined to make something of himself so that "when South Africa is free," he might return as well-equipped to build as he then was to destroy. In Canada, he found the bitter pill of multiculturalism. "Multiculturalism is racism multiplied," your father says. Your father, who learned so much in nearly twenty years of exile, finds himself accused of plagiarism. How could he know so much, so well? when he tries to explain why *The Heart of Darkness* poses some problems for the African mind.

He hopes that a university education and Canadian citizenship become other ways in which to engage in the struggle. Public speaking, performance poetry, story-telling are more lines in the weave of "the struggle." Curiously, it is in Canada that *ntate* moves beyond the deadly divisions of South African politics. He learns to count the African National Congress's Mafika Ludidi as friend, as well as Jacob Motswaledi, burning with Black Consciousness Movement's passion. Remember, *puna*, Jacob, whom you, as a two-year-old, also called "*puna*," and who patiently took you everywhere you asked including South African poet, Don Mattera's Halifax reading in 1992? Mattera too is BCM, the powerful and parallel philosophy and practice of African empowerment, which is not modeled on that of Malcolm X, Martin Luther King, Jr. or Stokely Carmichael. I have to say that, *puna*, since so many people cannot believe that Bantu Steven Biko's thought is original.

For his first two years in Canada, *ntate* could not speak his language. There was no one who spoke any of his African languages, let alone Sesotho, and he could not telephone his family since in the past phone calls had brought the Boer harassing his mother nightly for months. So you remember, *puna*, *ntate* telling you how *Rakadi Bopi* travelled to Zimbabwe to give the Ramphore ancestors' blessing to him before he came to Canada? *Ntate* came to see the political expediency of WUSC's[3] "throwing him" in the isolated University College of Cape Breton, both as a regional development initiative and as a barrier to exiled South Africans' political work. *Ntate* — revolutionary, poet, linguist, soldier, organic intellectual, sculptor, actor, musician, singer — "an African man, *puna*," he often said. However, the 1994 return to South Africa, as with so many cadres, was devastating; the South Africa of "the struggle" no longer exists. Your father did not know how to be in the "new" South Africa and became homeless again.

Ntate, who, in Audre Lorde's words, "was never meant to survive" plants the seed in an ostensibly barren *Acadienne* woman and, to our wonderment, the spirits sent you to us, *puna*. "We are making miracles," *ntate* said. Musing about why I had chosen to marry an African man and bear his child, one of my students said that it must have been this experience that shaped Mamma's race consciousness. "No," contradicted a Black student, "I think it's the other way around; it was her race consciousness that led her to marry an African man and bear his child." Actually, it's both, *puna*, for I never really understood racism until I had you.

For the first two years of your life, *ntate* was all of Africa to you, and he gave himself to your care. "You must bend the branch when it is green, *mma-rakgwedi*," he would say to me. He is your father who assisted your birth, confounding cultural taboo, to hold you warm from my body. He is your father who always had you in hands, a true African child. He is *ntate* who bathed you, changed you, fed you, sang to you freedom songs from the camps. Your favourite seemed to be a lament for Robert Sobukwe,[4] *Sobukwe, khaosi kokekhle...* In 1998, I took your picture, *puna*, as you stood outside Sobukwe's house on Robben Island. Remember, we took a hydrofoil boat there and, on the way, everyone was somewhat festive. On our return trip, there was silence, following the tour, led by one of *ntate's* cadres, who had been imprisoned there on Robben Island for four years. We have a picture of you with him outside the prison walls. He called you "a fine young man," and asked you to greet *ntate* for him when we got to Pretoria.

The Boers segregated all political prisoners from the general population but so feared the influence of Robert Sobukwe that they built a prison house for him, well removed from the main prison. It is said that Sobukwe was poisoned. The Boers put political prisoners on Robben Island, hoping, I suppose, that the dank Atlantic cold and gypsum quarry work would finish them off. *Mahdiba's*[5] eyesight was ruined working in that quarry. Nova Scotia's *Four The Moment* sing, "Dark crow caws bitter blue; yes, a bear brown, black and bitter blue; it's the only song, it knows how to use; for a nigger miner digging gypsum for the cash to fix his shoes." The weave comes full circle so many times, *puna*.

Ntate insisted that baby (you) have the best because these were things he could never have given to his first-born, your brother in Zimbabwe. You must have the best, because "you deserve," he said. He is your father, the African Canadian who turns his back on Canada, "the promised land." He decides that if he is to be challenged to show his papers in an airport lounge, it might as well be in South Africa. *Ntate* decides that the "empty smiles" of Canadians are to be avoided. *Ntate* dismisses the Americanization of Black Canadians, Black Caribbeans, Black Americans, and their rejection of Africa. "They are not conscious," he says. Your father comes to realize that in Canada, as in South Africa, he is still a *"kaffir."*

I have come to the end of the story, for now, *puna*. Where does this leave you, whose little brown body and naming so seriously disrupt what it means to be Canadian? I brought you to *Toronto, "the place of meeting,"* because I could not bring you up in South Africa; I was too afraid. Even now, on our visits, it is as if I can only breathe with relief when the plane touches down at Pearson Airport. Apartheid lives on in the "white country with a Black president," and the violence of apartheid is now unleashed everywhere, not just contained in the townships. But we both know, don't we *puna*, that Toronto is fraught with peril for a Black child? However, that will be your story to tell one day, should you so choose.

Ke a leboa,[6]
Mamma

Endnotes

1. *Making Something Happen: The Experiences of Black People in Nova Scotia, 1780 - 1900* (1984); *Nova Scotia's Black Renaissance, 1968-1986* (1988).

2. The name given to the State President, in Afrikaans, by freedom fighters.

3. World University Service of Canada.

4. Robert Sobukwe's profound philosophy led to the 1959 break with the ANC and the formation of the PAC. It was the PAC which organized the demonstration against the pass laws, which culminated in the infamous *Sharpeville Massacre* of 1961 in which the South African police opened fire on the demonstrators, killing at least fifty and wounding about two hundred more. And, it is the date of the *Sharpeville Massacre*, March 8, which the UN used to designate the International Day for the Elimination of Racism, so hypocritically observed in Canada.

5. The term of affectionate respect for Nelson Mandela who spent nineteen of his twenty-seven-year sentence on Robben Island and chose to celebrate the millenium there.

6. In Sesotho, this is the expression by which one gives thanks.

Writing Hockey Thru Race:
Rethinking Black Hockey in Canada

Gamal Abdel Shehid

Maybe this wide country just stretches your life to a thinness just trying to take it in, trying to calculate in it what you must do.... It always takes long to come to what you have to say, you have to sweep this stretch of land up around your feet and point to the signs, pleat whole histories with pins in your mouth and guess at the fall of words. — Dionne Brand, 1997[1]

Currently, the dominant theme in the discussion of the health of Canadian literature, history, and hockey is death. In the past five years, numerous articles and books have lamented the death of Canadiana. In hockey, think of the recent publication of *The Death of Hockey*; in history, there is Jack Granatstein's (1998) book, entitled: *Who Killed Canadian History?* In literature, think about the controversies and discussions over CanLit, which culminated in the furor over the 1994 staging of Writing Thru Race, the first conference in Canada that brought together exclusively aboriginal and nonwhite writers to discuss the question of Canada and literature.[2]

The recurrence of the theme of death and disappearance in contemporary discussions of Canadian culture are not accidental. They are a result of serious dislocations within the national fabric at nearly every level. These dislocations might be defined as a "writing back" from Black and subaltern voices in the country. In every cultural sphere work emerges from Black, South Asian, Arab, and First Nations communities. In sports, it has meant that the nation's leading athletes are often not white: witness Titus Channer and Sherman Hamilton (basketball), Otis Grant (boxing), Philomena Mensah and Donovan Bailey (track and field), Paul Kariya (hockey),

Emmanuel Sandhu (figure skating).

In this chapter, I attempt to speak to the gap between the mourning of Canadiana and a new wave of sporting stars and what it has meant for Black popular culture in Canada. Specifically, I attempt to evaluate the recent boom in literature concerning Black hockey players. First, I offer a look at some key Canadian texts on hockey written over the past thirty years to show how prevalent talk about hockey is to talk about death. I then suggest that representing hockey as dying produces a group of "villains" who are said to be killing hockey. Second, I read the work of Dionne Brand in relation to recent controversies about how race disrupts the Canadian literary canon (CanLit) as a way to rethink race and nation in Canada. Third, I consider Herb Carnegie's latest book, *A Fly in a Pail of Milk*, as well as the current writing on Black hockey players, most recently the focus on Willie O'Ree. In that section, I ask how equating O'Ree with Jackie Robinson might help us resist the death of hockey narrative. In the final section, I consider what it might mean to read and write hockey thru race, and suggest how such a writing subverts the common narrative on hockey, as well as disturbs some commonsensical notions of what Blackness signifies in Canada.

Representing Hockey

The connection between political change and discourses of hockey has been made by Gruneau and Whitson, who note that

> At the very moment that Canada is itself in question, and new voices are clamouring to have their identities recognized, many of hockey's deeply rooted meanings, traditions and associated identities need to be reassessed (1993: 7).

Gruneau and Whitson stress the indispensable nature of a critique of the mythologizing of hockey in popular culture. They note that "hockey deserves a prominent place in Canadian cultural studies" (1993:6). Speaking in favour of a constructionist view of hockey, they note that:

> there is something to be said for the argument that hockey draws on and dramatizes the Canadian experience with long winters, the cold and large open spaces. The problem arises

when Canadians' appreciation for hockey is mistaken for "nature" rather than something that is socially and culturally produced (1994: 26).

Gruneau and Whitson are correct in resisting a naturalization of hockey and in trying to think about how it works through popular culture. This view opens the way for a reading of hockey as a kind of national narrative.

There are three important elements to mythical hockey narratives in Canada. First, hockey is seen as the equivalent of Canada, or more specifically, the Canadian winter. Second, hockey is often described as timeless, a game that knows no history. Third, and this will be the main focus, hockey is (in recent memory) always represented as dead or dying. Ken Dryden and MacGregor begin their book, *Home Game*, in the following way:

Hockey is part of life in Canada. Thousands play it, millions follow it, and millions more surely try their best to ignore it altogether. But if they do, their disregard must be purposeful, done in conscious escape.... In Canada, hockey is one of winter's expectations (1989: 9).

According to Bruce Kidd and John MacFarlane:

hockey captures the essence of the Canadian experience in the New World. In a land so inescapably cold, hockey is the dance of life, an affirmation that despite the deathly chill of winter we are alive (1973:4).

In addition to its invigorating qualities and its ability to allow Canadians to survive the winter, hockey represents the absolute and discernible difference between Canadians and "our" neighbours, the Americans. Once again, Kidd and MacFarlane:

Hockey players like (Gordie) Howe are everything that actors like Paul Newman, television stars like Johnny Carson, and athletes like Joe Namath, Muhammad Ali, Johnny Bench and Arnold Palmer are for Americans (1972: 12).

It may come as no surprise that if hockey is seen as having this degree of significance within Canada, anything that threatens its hegemony might be the cause of anxiety. For example, as I wrote this chapter, the *Globe and Mail*'s sports page, as well as the CBC, were covering the Open Ice conference being held in Toronto to discuss hockey's future in Canada. The Open Ice conference, with Wayne Gretzky as its honorary chairman, had been convened to assess Canada's place in the hierarchy of world hockey. The news coverage of the conference reproduces the theme of death with the following headline: "Losing edge on world ice, Canadians feel"; and with a column by *Globe and Mail* columnist Stephen Brunt entitled "Is hockey losing hallowed stature?"[3]

In this brief example, we can see how hockey, death and loss are interconnected. The theme is so pervasive that "The Death of Hockey" is the title of two books on the subject of hockey, the first from 1973 by Kidd and MacFarlane, and the second written by Klein and Reif in 1998. Both books examine hockey's disappearance and death at the hands of a series of villains, and the danger of it being taken away. In the first, the enemy is the Americans, who have taken the innocent and childlike game of hockey out from under "our" feet. The authors argue that the death of hockey is accelerated "by our proximity to the United States and our cheap faith in free enterprise."[4] Moreover, they suggest that

> if hockey is a metaphor for what is right with Canada, it is also a metaphor for what is wrong. Hockey has come to symbolize our capitulation to economic realities as surely as it does our triumph over the physical ones (1973: 15).

The death of hockey, and the way that Canada is imagined to be faltering in such representations, automatically names a series of villains who are threatening to kill hockey. These villains, it will be shown, are any form of masculinity marked as effeminate, and any form of popular culture marked as "foreign" or homosexual. For example, *Home Game*, is largely about detailing the decline of enrollments in minor hockey across the country, and how Canadian kids are moving into "new" pursuits. In response to these "changes," the authors explain:

Many people have chosen to do other things. There are now dozens of other activities to capture the interest of the Saskatoon child and his or her parents, from Suzuki violin lessons to French lessons to gymnastics (1983: 50).

What is interesting in this formulation is how foreignness, and alternative masculinities, are united and positioned against hockey. Violin lessons, French lessons and gymnastics are not typical of a rugged Canadian masculinity. The kind of virility that requires one to brave the elements is at odds with the effete masculinity involved in playing the violin or speaking French.[5]

In addition, the vision of hockey as home put forward by Dryden, MacGregor, Kidd and MacFarlane relies upon a nostalgic version of Canada. But this vision can be deployed against threats to the notion that Canada, and by extension, hockey, is a fundamentally good and noble place. Laura Robinson notes:

> Hockey, as a sport, as a game played in the richness of Canadian winters, can be a beautiful and wonderful thing. But what happens in the name of team loyalty and in the tradition of "masculinity" has nothing to do with a great game of hockey. It is about men who use boys for their own sport (1998: 97).

Robinson's book *Crossing the Line* only works if we construct hockey as dying and, more importantly, if we construct a true hockey masculinity as straight. While she purports to be looking at violence against women in hockey, Robinson merely manipulates common sense homophobia to reinforce the nationalist narrative. She does so by using the stereotype of the gay male as inveterate sexual predator to tell the story of innocent young boys being preyed upon. This is a misleading and dangerous portrayal for a number of reasons. The most disturbing consequence of Robinson's portrayal is that she equates the systemic misogyny of hockey cultures with the clearly infrequent appearance of male (homosexual) pedophiles. She does this by summoning both as evidence of a deformed "masculinity" that is destroying the game (1998: 97). In addition to the incongruity of her comparison, this portrayal says nothing about young boys' own sexual choices, and continues to read homosexuality as an evil — not as an autonomous desire for boys and girls. Robinson says nothing about homosexuality in hockey other than through the paranoid criminalizing of Graham James.

Furthermore, Robinson says nothing of the homophobia that is constituitive of both men's and women's hockey. We are to believe, instead, that the problem is straight boys being preyed upon by their coaches, with no mention of the way that most hockey coaches, players, parents, and league officials spend much energy reproducing conventional heterosexual gender codes, and punish those who do not respond to them. Robinson's vilification of James secures her argument, but it also allows for a book with purported feminist intentions to bond with the machismo in the books by Kidd and MacFarlane, Dryden and MacGregor and Cherry. She does this by producing hockey's villains as queer. Moreover, it suggests the other side of the death of hockey, namely the persistent criminalizing of others in order to sustain panic and anxiety around the death of hockey. Far from hockey being the game and institution that produces a brutal white masculinity, hockey becomes the innocent victim of homosexuals who "threaten" the game.[6]

A Fly in a Pail of Milk

Writing thru race stages the eruption of cultural difference, or "other" scenes within the liberal nation, without claiming the privilege to alone represent that scene. Writing thru race haunts the nation with its other which it cannot possess. Instead, the nation is possessed; history calls forth its debts otherwise.[7]

Thus, homophobia (in Robinson), xenophobia (Dryden and MacGregor) and anti-Americanism (Kidd and MacFarlane) ground the traditional writing of hockey. To write about hockey in the normative sense is to deploy these kinds of exclusions, to not tolerate voices marked as different speaking back. Just like queer is unable to speak within Robinson's text, and the impossibility of a "foreign" (Suzuki violin playing) goalie for Dryden and MacGregor, Black speech is also impossible within these narratives. In fact, very few works on hockey reference Black, First Nations and other nonwhite peoples directly. To her credit, Robinson discusses racism in hockey in the conclusion, however briefly. But she also adopts a primitivist position with respect to First Nations people, suggesting that they provide a more gentle version of masculinity, which whites could learn from. Thus, once again, hockey's others are spoken for and are in no way integrated into the text.

Thus, writing hockey thru race is urgent work. In the following section, I look at what it might take to reconsider hockey from a point of view that does not centre on death, and by extension, whiteness. One way to begin is to think about Herb Carnegie's *A Fly in A Pail of Milk*. Carnegie, a well-known and highly skilled Black hockey player in the 1940s and 1950s, was prevented from playing in the National Hockey League because of racism. Carnegie was undoubtedly as good as or better than most of the great hockey players of his era. Disbarred from the NHL, he played on a number of "minor" league teams, most of which were in Quebec. While in Quebec, he played on a team in Shawinigan Falls on an all-Black line-up that also included Manny McIntyre from Fredericton, New Brunswick, and Ossie Carnegie, Herb's brother.

Carnegie's book, a popular autobiography published in 1998, is the first book-length manuscript to deal with racism in hockey, and therefore, it is a very significant book. While the book ends on a disappointingly liberal note, encouraging kids to overcome obstacles, what the book has to say about racism in Canadian hockey is unflinching. Carnegie's work is different from the traditional hockey writing in that he doesn't need to reproduce cliches about Canadiana in order to support his claims.

On occasion, Carnegie does presume a raceless Canadian identity; however, this is infrequent. He notes:

I wasn't a coloured kid, I was a Canadian kid who dreamed just like other Canadian boys of playing in the NHL.... My dream would not come true, not because of a lack of talent or a willingness to work hard, but because of racism (1998: 113).

In spite of this attempt at racelessness, most of the book is unsympathetic to racism in Canada. While Carnegie's story should hardly surprise, its documentation of the cultural politics of race in Canada is important. This work helps us think about how much or how little difference the national narrative can handle. Interestingly, the hockey narrative of innocent young boys being preyed upon by foreigners, homosexuals and greedy Americans does not appear in Carnegie's work. In fact, the death of hockey in no way organizes Carnegie's memoir. For Carnegie, the death of hockey is a different thing altogether: white racism becomes the death of NHL hockey for Carnegie, his brother Ossie and a host of Black and Native hockey players.

Instead of hockey's death as the central theme, the memoir is organized around a love for hockey, in spite of the kinds of discrimination that he faced. Carnegie's investment in hockey and competition is heavy, which opens up the space to talk about hockey differently. Moreover, it suggests that questions of Blackness and hockey are not recent or external issues but organic to several Black cultures in Canada. A *Fly in a Pail of Milk* is an example of a text that begins to write hockey thru race and open up our consciousness beyond myth. In addition, it is indispensable to the project of mapping Black desires and identifications in sporting cultures.

Thus, Carnegie's memoir refuses the structure of official hockey narratives, which is to say that it exposes them as falsehoods and commercials for nation. But in addition to responding to whiteness, we must consider what this work does to our own thinking about Blackness and sport in Canada. The question in reading Carnegie's book is: how does it enable one to think Blackness differently?

The Jackie Robinson of Hockey?

The telling of hockey history through its minoritarian elements expands the cultural files of the game and the potential for new subject formations that are not limited by the standard account.[8]

Herb Carnegie's biography does not emerge from a vacuum. It is part of a wave of recent writing and broadcasting on Black hockey players. Part of this Black hockey renaissance has to do with the popularity and emergence of a number of Black hockey stars in Canada currently in the NHL, such as Jarome Iginla, Mike Grier, and Anson Carter. Previously, it was almost impossible to find work on the subject, this is no longer the case. First, Gary Genosko's recent work has unearthed some of the important contributions of Black hockey players. Second, in 1997, CBC Radio aired a two-part documentary on racism in hockey, entitled *Black Ice*. Third, academics have now begun to study Black hockey players. For example, at the 1998 annual conference of the North American Association for Sports History, the first paper in the association's history on Black hockey players was given by Brad Brady. In fact, the NHL has jumped on the bandwagon in recent years, with a Diversity Task Force, with Willie O'Ree as the chair, in an attempt to "encourage" Black and other nonwhite hockey players to play hockey.

O'Ree was the first Black hockey player in the NHL, who began playing with the Boston Bruins in 1958. Genosko notes:

> O'Ree's career was mostly spent in the minors playing for Western hockey league teams in Los Angeles and San Diego. Despite the obscurity that such a career path normally entails, he is widely known as "the Jackie Robinson of hockey" (1999: 144).

However, while some scholars, including Genosko, appear to uncritically accept this narrative of Black participation in hockey, and its attendant need for a "Jackie Robinson," I question what it means to read O'Ree in this way, given Canadian narratives' inability to allow Blackness to speak for itself. More specifically, my question is how does a discourse of the "Jackie Robinson of hockey" resist and subvert the dominant narrative of hockey, which represents hockey as dying. My concerns also apply to Herb Carnegie's memoir, and to those who wish to read Carnegie in the same celebratory light as O'Ree.

There are several difficulties with calling O'Ree the Jackie Robinson of hockey. First, it is another example of attempts to read Blackness, in this case a largely Canadian Blackness, through an American lens. While I am not doubting the influence of American popular culture in Canada, and the Maritimes more specifically, there is clearly a different political and cultural history to attend to.[9] In Canada, while coloured hockey associations go as far back as the late 1800s,[10] there were no "Negro Leagues" as there were in American baseball.[11] Moreover, because of differences in the way that racism was structured in the United States, the fanfare and hype surrounding Robinson's entry into Major League (read: white) baseball was in no way the same as it was for O'Ree to enter the NHL.

In addition to the problem of historical specificity, there is a politcal problem with reading Willie O'Ree through Jackie Robinson and the surrounding mythology. The liberal foundations that such a reading demands are clearly insufficient to rethinking hockey beyond the death narrative. In its most conservative form, what I call the Jackie Robinson narrative goes like this.[12] First, American racism previously prevented Blacks from playing baseball in white leagues. Yet through the goodness of liberal Branch Rickey, Robinson got a shot with the Brooklyn Dodgers. And, in spite of constant racism and harassment, Robinson persevered and became a star, embraced by white and Black fans alike.

There are a few foundational assumptions here worth underlining. First, the myth relies on the assumption that Robinson's being a star in the Major Leagues is somehow more valid than his being a star in the Negro Leagues, which automatically privileges the white leagues. This construction overlooks the fact that many Black baseball stars refused promotions to Major League baseball teams because they felt that they had nothing to prove.[13] Second, while it is clear that Branch Rickey was somewhat liberal, albeit in a very entrepreneurial way, his role in the events leading up to Robinson's signing with the Dodgers is generalized, so that the fantasy of liberal whites helping Black players seems to be the only way to fight racism. This has the effect of once again suggesting that white people have been at the forefront of the fight against racism. Third, perseverance and hard work, classically individualist values, get prioritized over anti-racism, and other forms of collective response to injustice. For this reason, Jackie Robinson becomes an American hero in a way that Paul Robeson, for example, could never have been. In fact, Robinson was the star witness testifying against Robeson at Robeson's appearance before the House of UnAmerican Activities Committee in 1949.[14]

These foundations are what makes the facile deployment of a Jackie Robinson narrative by people like Bill Clinton, Major League Baseball and the NHL possible; yet they are deeply disturbing. This means that one must think twice before applying this narrative to any context, whether to baseball in the United States or to hockey and the NHL. In the context of hockey, it is troubling how easily such a narrative can coexist with official forms of talk about hockey. Recall the way that Blackness and alterity worked in the death of hockey narratives: they were either vilified, absent, or taken as examples of a lost humanity. In all cases, they were merely tangential to hockey, in which a white core was presumed to be real, timeless and truly Canadian. The question worth considering is in what way does the deployment of Willie O'Ree as Jackie Robinson get at these problems? The answer, unfortunately, is hardly at all. Blackness is once again spoken for — it becomes an add-on; and because the myth of Jackie Robinson is all about soothing racist egos, the narrative can coexist with the death of hockey narrative since it in no way attacks the white core that is presumed to be foundational to hockey.

Remapping Hockey Thru Literature: Dionne Brand

In the beginning of this essay, I noted that similar anxieties about the varied deaths of Canadiana occur within debates about hockey, history, and literature. Hence, some of the contributions made in other debates might prove useful in trying to think about hockey differently. Recently, several theorists have written about the failure of discourses of Canadian nationalism from the point of view of Blackness and/or subaltern positions.[15] Dionne Brand's critique of nationalism and her insights regarding speaking back to nation are indispensable in the context of hockey.

One important concept in Brand's critique of nationalism is the way that loss and forgetting are represented in Canadian cultural politics. Brand has discussed how, for immigrants, adopting a Canadian identity is contingent upon a loss of memory and a denial of history. She argues that Canadian identity involves forgetting one's pre-Canadian identity, be it Portuguese, Rwandan, Somali, and so on. This loss of memory is necessary in order to adopt fantasies of Canadiana as better than those available where you might have come from. Brand writes:

All immigration is seen as fleeing a horrible past/place and arriving gratefully at an unblemished present/place. So Canada presents itself as an alluring historyless place, at least not a place charged with a similarly hostile history, even as one is persuaded later that it isn't, as one is presented with the pristine documents of it's not-where-you-come-from-but-better morality (1998: 138).

Brand goes on to note that this forgetting produces a kind of emptiness at the core of Canadian identity, which she refers to as an "absent presence":

This absent presence is at the core of Canadian identity, a

whole set of people relegated to a present past. An emptying out of the past, then, both physical and mental, seems to be crucial to the concept (1998: 139).

We might think of hockey narratives in a similar fashion to this description of the "absent presence" within Canadian identity. The death of hockey tradition is founded upon a white core, which, according to the authors cited, is under constant siege from a series of villains who presumably have not remembered to forget their past. This white core of hockey is similarly invested with notions of timelessness, historylessness, and, by extension, racelessness.

Disrupting this core requires many strategies. In another work, Brand articulates what it might mean to confront this loss of memory and to speak back to this absent presence. She theorizes what it might mean to speak from the position of the forgotten body, or from the subaltern body in Canada. The coming to voice of Black and other nonwhite selves, she notes, is a recognition of these overarching historical forces:

Maybe this wide country just stretches your life to a thinness just trying to take it in, trying to calculate in it what you must do.... It always takes long to come to what you have to say, you have to sweep this stretch of land up around your feet and point to the signs, pleat whole histories with pins in your mouth and guess at the fall of words.[16]

Speaking and living a different Canada flies in the face of official narratives of what this land is like, and who lives here. The difficulty Brand has with speech, as it is constructed through nation, are anathema to ardent Canadian nationalists and to the predominant form of writing on hockey in this country. Such writers speak with an almost inconceivable ease about what and who are meant by Canada and Canadians. Brand seems to suggest that new languages are necessary in order to remap oneself and rewrite the nation.[17] Hence, adopting liberal and America-centric forms to narrate Blackness, as in the representation of O'Ree as hockey's Jackie Robinson, is also insufficient. Instead, Brand suggests that cacophony — something akin to the notion of patchwork — is what gets closest to our reality. Says Brand:

What would we create as a more realistic and life-respecting expression of our collectivity? Maybe riding the College streetcar; maybe it is an admission of our history, an admission of our collectivity; maybe it is many stories and not one dominating one (1998: 145).

Brand goes so far as to suggest that nation itself is a fantasy, and that any attempt to produce homogeneity will have its victims. In a poem entitled "Land to Light On," she writes:

You come to this, here's the marrow of it, not moving, not standing, it's too much to hold up, what I really want to say is, I don't want no fucking country, here or there or all the way back, I don't like it, none of it, easy as that. I'm giving up on land to light on, and why not, I can't perfect my own shadow, my violent sorrow, my individual wrists (1997: 48).

Far from inserting herself into a nationalist narrative, Brand marks the wounds that many of us suffer as a result of nation-state practices that seek to racialize and, at the same time, homogenize. I cite Brand to make a connection between the way racist fantasies of nation form a kind of language and what it might mean to speak back to them, especially in the context of writing Black hockey experiences in Canada. After we have let go of the tendency to read Black hockey through the lens of Jackie Robinson, and chart the "lost" history of Black hockey players — who have, after all, played all across this nation for over one hundred years, as have First Nations, Japanese Canadian and Chinese Canadian players — what other kinds of investigation do we need to do?

In trying to write back to this narrative, there are several possible places to go, which makes the current period of excitement around hockey and Blackness theoretically fruitful. To be sure, we might pay attention to Brand's underlining of the value of cacophony in rewriting hockey in this country. For if it is impossible to write the nation through a white monotone, doing so in a Black one is equally disturbing. We would then risk repeating tired Black clichés, of which the myth of Jackie Robinson is one.

One place to begin might be reinvestigating the fight over which kind of hockey became the dominant one at the turn of the twentieth century. At that time, there was a fight between two styles of play: the Montreal rules and the Halifax rules. The Montreal rules — a much more conservative style of play, which prevented forward passing — won out. We also know that the Halifax Leagues of the time had a number of Black hockey players, while there were fewer Black players in Montreal. As well as shoring up some of the documented history, one of the important questions here is: in what ways was Blackness a factor in the victory of the Montreal rules? Also, was there any way that the view that forward passing was too anti-Victorian was tied to the bodies of Black hockey players? These questions, and we may be able to think of others — like, what was the role of First Nations hockey players in these struggles — allow for thinking Blackness as organic to hockey, and present a subversive option to reading the nation. Such an investigation would remap Blackness and hockey in profoundly different ways from the dominant narrative.

Conclusion

This chapter has outlined how important hockey is to fantasies of Canadian nationalism. More specifically, I have shown how to talk about hockey is to talk about death, and how this form is central to many forms of nationalist description, such as those found in Canadian literature and history. The death of hockey works to perform what Roy Miki calls an act of "cultural territorialization," which relegates Blackness to the nation's margins. The inability of the death of hockey narrative to deal with Blackness means that there is a tendency to Americanize Blackness as evidenced by my discussion of Willie O'Ree. The appropriations of Canadian Blackness into a liberal script originating in the United States is not new, but it does convey that the task at hand involves more than unearthing Black hockey players.

I have suggested one place to begin rewriting hockey thru race. By beginning with hockey at the turn of the century, I do not mean to suggest that older is better, only that thinking about Blackness and hockey does not have to be focussed on "firsts," nor does it have to always speak thru whiteness, as is too often the case. There are other examples, such as thinking about hockey's presence within Caribbean communities in Toronto and its suburbs from the late 1960s to the present. There are plenty of places to begin — and lots of work to do.

Works Cited

Brand, D. 1998. *Bread Out of Stone*. Toronto: Vintage Canada.

Brand, D. 1997. *Land to Light On*. Toronto: McClelland and Stewart.

Carnegie, H. 1997. *A Fly in a Pail of Milk*. Oakville: Mosaic Press.

Dryden, K. and MacGregor, R. 1989. *Home Game: Hockey and Life in Canada*. Toronto: McClelland and Stewart.

Duberman, M. 1988. *Paul Robeson*. New York: Alfred A. Knopf.

Etue, E. and Williams, M. K., 1996. *On the edge: women making hockey history*. Toronto: Second Story Press.

Gruneau, R. and Whitson, D. 1993. *Hockey Night in Canada: Sport, Identities and Cultural Politics*. Toronto: Garamond Press.

Kidd, B. and MacFarlane, J. 1972. *The Death of Hockey*. Toronto: New Press.

Klein, J.Z. and Reif, K. 1998. *The Death of Hockey*. Toronto: Macmillan.

McFarlane, S. 1995. "The Haunt of Race: Canada's Multiculturalism Act, the Politics of Incorporation, and Writing Thru Race." In Fuse, vol 18, 3. 18-31.

Miki, R. 1998. *Broken Entries*. Toronto: Mercury Press

Rampersad, A. 1997. *Jackie Robinson*. New York: Alfred A. Knopf.

Robinson, L. 1998. *Crossing the Line*. Toronto: McClelland and Stewart.

Silvera, M. 1989. *Silenced*. Toronto: Sister Vision.

Walcott, R. 1997. *Black Like Who?* Toronto: Insomniac Press.

Endnotes

1. Dionne Brand, 1997: 43.

2. There have been other, similar conferences. See McFarlane, 1995.

3. *Globe and Mail*, August 25, 1999, S1.

4. As cited in Gruneau and Whitson: 26.

5. Note that this economy does not work if we are talking about girls. What this suggests it that the authors were using "people" to mean young boys.

6. For a more nuanced treatment of issues around sexuality and hockey, with respect to women's hockey, please see Etue and Williams, 1996.

7. Scott MacFarlane, 1995: 20.

8. Genosko, 1999: 145.

9. Willie O'Ree is from Fredericton, New Brunswick.

10. See Gruneau and Whitson, Chapter 2.

11. One fact worth noting in comparing O'Ree and Robinson is that both had to cross the border to begin their careers. Robinson, an American, came to Montreal; O'Ree, a Canadian, went to Boston.

12. Clearly, Jackie Robinson's life is caricatured within this narrative. For a more in-depth biography of Robinson, see Arnold Rampersad, 1997. However, it is worth noting that Robinson himself responded to and attempted to embody the media stereotype in his life, which the Rampersad biography implies.

13. In addition, Negro League stars at the time were very highly paid, and would have had to accept salary reductions to play in the Major Leagues.

14. For more on this, see Duberman, 1989.

15. Examples of this work are Walcott, 1997; Miki, 1998; Silvera, 1989.

16. Dionne Brand, 1997: 43.

17. For more on the relationship between Brand and language, please see Walcott, 1997, Chapter 5. Walcott suggests that: "What Brand's...poetry suggests to me is how the language used by diasporic Black people references both their doubled existences, and also existences that refuse foundations (112)."

"Canadianizing" Blackness:
Resisting the Political

David Sealy

The future of Black intellectual life lies neither in a deferential disposition toward the Western parent nor in a nostalgic search for the African one. Rather it resides in a critical negation, wise preservation and insurgent transformation of the Black lineage which protects the earth and projects a better world.
— Cornell West, 1998[1]

I doubted if any Black from the diaspora could really return to Africa. — Maya Angelou, 1996[2]

Blackness as a sign is never enough. What does the Black subject do, how does it act, how does it think politically... being Black isn't really enough for me: I want to know what your cultural politics are. — Stuart Hall, 1992[3]

Canada is a country more interested in "computers" than "racial justice." [4]

In the introduction to *Frontiers: Essays and Writings on Racism and Culture* Marlene Nourbese Philip states:

There has been times when I thought the unthinkable — that it is less cruel to kill a people leaving their culture and respect intact than to denude them of their culture and by various means deride and destroy it, leaving them to howl their pain and anger down through the centuries. And isn't this partly what Los Angeles and Toronto, and before that Miami and before that Watts, and before that the Haitian revolution and before that — have been all about? *The howling of our pain at the anger of our loss of culture* [my emphasis].[5]

In his essay "Towards a Future That Has No Past," Orlando Patterson comes to the following conclusion concerning Black people in the Americas:

The Blacks now face a historic choice. To survive they must abandon any search for a past, must indeed recognize that they lack any claims to a distinctive cultural heritage, and that the path ahead lies not in myth making and in historical reconstruction, which are always doomed to failure but in accepting the epic challenge of their reality. *Blacks[s].. can be the first group in the history of mankind to transcend the confines and grip of a cultural heritage,* and in so doing they can become the most truly modern of all people — a people who feel no need for a nation a past or a particularistic culture, but whose style of life will be rational and continually changing adoption to the exigencies of survival at the highest possible level of existence [my emphasis].[6]

Three young Black women from Toronto journey to the site of the filming of the African American woman filmmaker Julie Dash's *Daughter of the Dust* as if conducting a pilgrimage to the site of the enactment of their Black femaleness. A young Black female graduate student is told by her white professor that there are no "political" Black female organizations worthy researching in the Windsor area. Young Black students at York University, born and raised in Toronto, are constantly questioned as to their island of origin. A young Black man living in Toronto for the past fifteen years is accused of a crime and there is talk of deporting him to Jamaica, the place of his birth. A well-known Ottawa radio host suggests on a call-in show that perhaps some of these young Black "criminals" do not deserve Canadian citizenship. An English professor at a well-known Canadian University tells her students that when she told her friends in Sweden that she was emigrating to Canada, they said that Canada was better than the United States as "there are no Blacks in Canada." What is the connection between these narratives, Nourbese Philip's discussion of "loss of culture," Orlando Patterson's claims about "cultural transcendence," and hegemonic constructions of Blackness in Canada on the cusp of the twenty-first century?

Of course, these questions involve competing interpretations of history, nation, coloniality, postcoloniality, Black identity and culture within modern and postmodern Canada, which cannot all be addressed here. Let me, however, briefly outline some of the basic contours of this discussion by proceeding through a more direct route. I would like to sketch a provisional "reading" of Black Canadian identity, which to come to terms with all these diverse constructions of Canadian Blackness. My reading takes as its starting point the differential histories of Black peoples in Canada, while allowing for an understanding of "border-crossing" as an integral feature of Black diasporic life. I therefore resist viewing Black Canadian life as either a repetition of Black American life, Black African life or Black Caribbean life.[7]

I am not at all dismissing constructions of Black Canadian life as directly connected to the histories of the peoples of the African diaspora. Rather, I want to suggest that discussions that centre on African authenticity or African personality elide the diversity of Black diasporic histories, and with it "the diverse ways in which Black diasporic subjects have selectively appropriated, incorporated, European ideologies, culture and institutions, alongside an "African" heritage."[8] The search for an originary univocal "Black" and or "African" source precludes the plurivocality of "Blackness." What has come to be named Blackness is therefore not the product of some pure "Africanness," but of

> partial synchronization, of engagement across cultural boundaries, of the confluence of more than one cultural tradition, of the negotiations of subordinate and dominant positions, of the subterranean strategies of recoding and transcoding, of critical signification and signifying... hybridized from a vernacular base.[9]

Here it is important to make the separation between, on the one hand, what has come to be called "Afrocentricity," as promulgated by Molefi Asante, and the "Pan-Africanism" of C.L.R. James and George Padmore; and on the other, what Paul Gilroy calls distinguishing "between the contemporary versions of Black nationalism and that of the past."[10] The dehistorizing and essentializing of Black identity into "their traditions versus ours" not only ignores the multiplicity of social relations within which Black people (gender, nationality, class, vicinity, et cetera) are inscribed, but also valorizes the very ground of the racism we are trying to deconstruct.[11] It is therefore the terms of this plural "Blackness" that is at stake within these discussions, never some essential "Blackness" or "Africanness." These discussions are therefore always political, and reflect the concrete and often contradictory sites in which Black people find themselves in their daily lives, and the potential for inventing ways of successfully transforming these sites. These discussions inevitably, in turn, involve questions of power and possibilities.

Part I

I want to begin following Stuart Hall and Paul Gilroy by suggesting that the very idea of "Blackness" is integral to what is modern. The very notion of "Blackness" is caught up in the series of events, movements, appropriations, translations involved in the development of capitalism and the nation-state — all of which partially make up the modern.

This modernity can be characterized as the movement from a hierarchically defined, organic premodern episteme, where the self is defined in terms of the role one is born into (i.e., king, peasant, et cetera), in a hierarchically defined order, to a differentially defined modern episteme, where the self is defined in terms of essential rational agency. In the former episteme, human agency was proscribed within the parameters of one's place within the order of things. In the latter, human agency is proscribed within the parameters of rational subjectivity.

According to this grand modern narrative, a self is a being capable of rational reflections on his or her actions and world.[12] The essence of the modern political revolution, then, was the extension of full and equal moral treatment to all beings capable of rational reflection on their actions and the world.

To be moral within the premodern narrative would be to abide by the tenements of an atemporal, prescribed set of norms, which proscribe activity in terms of one's place in the order. To act morally would be to act in accordance with standards delineated by the conditions that pertain to one's prescribed place in the "Great Chain of Being."

With modernity, however, a shift occurs, as church is separated from state, reason is separated from a transcendent, prescribed moral order, and subjectivity is separated from role. Thus, truth and justice are no longer to be found within a rigid moral order, but in the free, rational, and self-conscious subject.

At the centre of modernity's critique of the premodern episteme is faith in human reason. In a statement exemplary of modern faith in rationality, Kant declares: "Have courage to use your own reason! This is the motto of the enlightenment." The authority previously invested in the premodern order becomes internalized in "man," and "heteronomy becomes autonomy as the words of one become the voice of all." Each rational free subject therefore has a duty to abide by the governance of rationality. Good judgement is therefore exercised in terms of universal public standards of rationality. Each rational agent can thus appeal to the same universal standards in judging action. And each judgement can always be subjected to rational considerations. Each subject is free to reason in whatever way he or she judges fit, the parameters of his or her reasoning being the standard of rationality itself. Thus, each subject, in so far as he is rational, is equal and free. Self-conscious subjectivity, as free rational agency, is therefore the arbiter of truth and knowledge. Rational self-consciousness, not a prescribed position or condition, delimits and determines the terms of equality and freedom.

Political equality, democracy, and liberal rights, including the right to private contracting, are therefore correspondent extensions of this monological ontology of the modern self. Following this reasoning, those incapable of rational and impartial reflection on their self and their world cannot be accorded equal moral treatment. Furthermore, those incapable, for whatever reason, of rational reflection on their action and the world, must for their own good be stewarded or controlled until such a time as they learn how to be rational reflective agents.

Under the modern paradigm, then, the Black self was considered "naturally" incapable of rational reflection on its actions and world, as the Black self had not yet achieved the status of rational subjectivity.[13] Or exemplary selfhood (self-consciousness) and, therefore, could not be accorded equal moral treatment. The Black self was therefore seen to be at a "prehuman," irrational stage of development, incapable of being the *subject* of its own life; it must therefore become the *object* of another's life, only to be stewarded into true rational selfhood and humanness.[14]

The same rationality that supposedly frees humanity from a hierarchically defined order becomes the grounds for exclusion of Black subjects. Constructed in this way, Blackness personifies degraded otherness, exemplify radical alterity, and embodies alien difference.[15] Blackness is thus the ultimate other: the excesses of modernity, whiteness its norm. Political equality therefore could not, in the modern arena, be extended to the Black self. However, even through considerations of race and gender were ostensibly inessential to the modernist universal personhood, the subject of the modernist project turned out, not surprisingly, to be exclusively white, male, European, and bourgeois. Modernity invents an ontology of equal, free, and self-conscious agency and democracy, only to deny it to, among others, Black subjects.

Furthermore, one of the features that marks late modernity (especially since the Vietnam War), in its most developed form, is the postmodern, the so-called decentring of the grand narratives and the accompanying "shifting of terrain of culture toward popular practices, toward everyday practices, toward local narratives, toward the decentring of the old hierarchies and the grand narratives."[16] What emerges out of this decentring of grand Western narratives of control and mastery is the narrative of difference and voice, which emphasizes contingency, particularity, partiality, and context — what could be called the excesses of modernity. The postmodern can therefore be said to be well on the way with the decentring of whiteness — where whiteness as plenitude is shown to be constituted by Blackness as lack. That is, whiteness as the full embodiment of universal rational free agency, is constituted by the erasure of Black particularity. Cornel West states that "to take seriously the multileveled oppression of [Black] peoples is to raise crucial questions regarding the conditions for the possibility of the modern West, the nature of European concepts of rationality."[17]

Here, I do not want to get embroiled in a discussion as to where or when the postmodern began or, for that matter, what is the source of this decentring of the Western grand narratives.[18] There is a sense in which the decentring of the Western grand narratives of truth, subjectivity, democracy, liberalism, rationality, and progress was happening from their very inception; particularly given the fact that these narratives were appropriated and translated by those on the periphery. For example, in early versions of the anti-colonial movements and the anti-slavery movement, modern notions of subjectivity, equality, democracy and rationality were appropriated as tools for the use of subordinated groups.

The demand of these groups was for the freedom accorded to the rational subjects to be extended to those constructed as irrational. There is, then, an ambivalence at the heart of modernity: in deconstructing premodern conceptions of a hierarchically transcendent order, and in positing rationality, freedom and equality as the essence of humanness, all the while ensuring that some are incapable of realizing this freedom, modernity allows for its own undoing since the subordinate can also claim rational, free agency.[19] As Chantal Mouffe has noted: "[a]ll positions that have been constructed as relations of domination/subordination will be deconstructed because of the subversive character of democratic discourse."[20]

> As long as equality has not yet acquired (with the democratic revolution) its place of central significance in the social imaginations of Western societies, struggles for this equality cannot exist. As soon as the principle of equality is admitted in one domain however, the eventual questioning of all forms of equality is the inevitable consequence.[21]

The same pattern emerges in both the early worker's movement and the early women's movement; and in, for example, the Haitian Revolution, where we see the translation and appropriation of the ideals of revolutionary "Jacobinism" — liberty, equality, and fraternity — into a slave revolution.

Each of these movements then appropriates and translates the modern ideal of democracy and political equality into a context which extends well beyond its traditional parameters. Blackness here now demands equal standing with whiteness.

In the period since World War II sometimes characterized as late capitalism, there has taken place a shift in difference politics, also called identity politics — a politics which combats the very terms of its naming. The assumption of voice by diverse groups with differing expressions of value in the political and cultural clash, opens up cracks in the hegemonic walls of standardized cultural identity. What emerges is a politics of identity that renegotiates the very terms of modernity. Again, as Mouffe has said of these "developments":

> Democracy extends its field of influence from its starting point, the equality of all citizens in political democracy, to socialism which extends equality to the level of the economy and then into other social relations, such as sexual, racial, generational and regional.[22]

To be specific, it is not simply that Blackness wants to be given equal standing to rational subjectivity, as with the assimilationist ideals of the earlier modern civil rights movement. Rather, Blackness utilizes the language of self-determination and self-actualization — for example, in the Black Power movement. Blackness takes its political fight away from the boardrooms and courts of the civil rights movement, and into the everyday reality of Black life, attempting along the way to frame uniquely Black political languages.

This shift from classical modern liberalism to what Richard Rorty calls "postmodern bourgeois liberalism" signals a shift from a public policy that ignored difference and particularity in the name of universal personhood to one that acknowledges difference and diversity in the name of pluralism. It is this postmodern context we see in Canada with the development of a discourse of Official Multiculturalism, now called "Heritage Canada," and visible minority public policy, where culture and race are deemed relevant considerations in formulating state public policy.

In and of themselves, these policies cannot be viewed as a version of the exact same invisibility, as they seem to partially broaden the conditions for the transgressing of the established radicalized spaces. However, they are also part of the commodification of every aspect of Black lives, a space characterized by Hall, who writes that: "I know that what replaces 'invisibility' is a kind of carefully regulated, segregated visibility."[23] But this "regulated" visibility cannot be dismissed outright (as in some zero-sum game) as "culture" is always a site of contestation. Following Marlene Nourbese Philip, we could suggest that "[m]ulticulturalism as we know it [may have] no answers for the problem of racism..." However, there can be no denying that the disavowal of the monocultural conception of nation and culture implied in multicultural discourse goes a long way in the fight against racism.[24]

Part 2

My reading of Black Canadian identity attempts to resist essentializing, dehistoricizing, and depoliticizing Black Canadian identity into either (1) simplistic notions of race representation for the use of the race management industry, or (2) into the visible minority nonesense that has at times become synonymous with much race discourse in Canada, or (3) into quasi-religious, romantic Africanist discourse that elides the differential histories of Black peoples in the New World. Further, my reading acknowledges the different subject positions in which each social agent is always inscribed, and the diverse possibilities for the construction of these subject positions. Thus, our Blackness or Black identity does not constitute all of us: we are always different, negotiating different kinds of differences — of gender, of sexuality, of class.[25]

What has come to be called "Canadian" identity does not simply rotate around different constructions of the so-called "French-English problem," "regional problems," "multi-culty" discourse, "the vertical mosaic" or "the just society." Rather, notions of Blackness and its relationship to Canada and Canadian identity is directly connected to the history of race talk and radicalized discourse in Canada "within the context of the emergence, development and decline of... capitalism." The oppression and domination of Black Canadians is a particular version of the racial problematic that emerges from — but is not limited to — the development and decline of British and French colonialism,their former white settler colony — Canada — and what Paul Gilroy has called the Black Atlantic.[26]

This history includes innumerable phenomena, such as the colonization and settlement of the so-called New World space called Canada both by British and French capitalist imperialism; the eventual defeat of the French forces; the founding of the Canadian nation-state coupled with systematic attempts to eliminate and colonize, i.e., rename aboriginal peoples. These processes were limited to the univocal naming of Canada and Canadian identity, from as early as the American revolutionary period, as an un-

American, or even anti-American space, which in turn constructed Canada as a site of Western European whiteness.[27]

The implication of this construction of Canadian identity for Black identity is revealing: it's impossible to be both Black and Canadian at the same time, since Canada is imagined either as a place without Black people, or where the few Blacks there are well-behaved, even apolitical. The connection looms large here between Blackness construed as "political" (in a post-civil-rights sense), and insurgent political activity and criminal activity.

The very calling of oneself as Black, the naming of the "Black Movement" itself, are reappropriations of a term of ultimate degradation to empower African diasporic peoples. The so-called "Black Movement" is a social movement of self-definition and actualization of Blackness, which counteracts and undermines the ways modernity has traditionally characterized Blackness. Implicit within a construction of a Canada without Blackness is a claim that there is not and has never been a Black movement in Canada. Black people, conceived in this Canadian sense, are well-behaved, passive subjects, unlikely to participate in the Black activist political stirrings of their sisters and brothers to the South. The name "Black" as a reappointed sign of political agency can not be applied to Black Canadians. The following appeared in the *Globe & Mail* in the latter part of 1969 — interestingly enough, just a few months after the now infamous Sir George Williams incident:

> Most Toronto Negroes [sic] are not militant. And they prefer the term Negro and coloured or Afro-American. *To a militant, Black is a political term* [my emphasis]. Generally it means an advocate of "Black Power," never call a militant coloured.[28]

The comparison here is between well-behaved and content Black Canadians and their "criminal and politically active," Black-American, and Black Third World counterparts. Canada is here construed as either an un-American or even anti-American space. According to this reasoning, "we" Canadians are better people than Americans, and therefore take better care or, at least, are better able to control, "our" Blacks than the American. Here we can see manifestations of what Michael Dorland has characterized as the quintessential Canadian response to modernity: resentment with a racist twist. As Kass Banning has stated:

> Dorlands cataloguing treatise on Canadian resentment suggests that the Canadian psyche displaces its multi-reasoned and well deserved feelings of inadequacy by eradicating difference.[29]

"Truly Canadian" Black Canadians see racial considerations in Canada as irrelevant, as there is little if any racism in Canada to protest. Black Canadians, unlike their Black American counterparts, have little to worry about, since Black people and white people live in harmony in Canada. Thus, wherever anti-racist political activity emerges among Black Canadians, it is part of the Americanization of Canada, something which Canadians have always actively resisted. The well-known Black activist Rocky Jones appearance on Halifax TV to assure viewers that there would be no Black Panther invasion of Nova Scotia — this "while the R.C.M.P. actually requested immigration authorities to stop any Negroes [sic] crossing the border" — is exemplary of this tendency.[30] The impetus for Black Canadian anti-racist political activity is always deemed to flow from sources outside the Canadian nation-state, and is therefore not related to any concrete Canadian situations.

On this manichaean construction of Black Canada, one can legitimately say that there were very few Black Canadian political organizations prior to the 1960s and 1970s migrations of Black people from the Caribbean. This follows since "authentic" Black Canadians are relatively passive, contented subjects, whereas much of Black "political" activity emerged within the rebellions and riots of Watts and Detroit; and more recently Brixton, Soweto or L.A. — this, even though attempts were made to export them to Canada in the post 1960s era. Following this reasoning, organizations such as the Black United Front in Nova Scotia, and even the now legendary National Black Canadian Coalition were attempts by Black Canadians to recast their own situation in light of the American reality — what we might call an illegitimate transmigration of racial metaphors.

But is there not a long history of Canadian racism, which Black Canadians are responding to? As Harry Arthurs, former President and Vice Chancellor of York University, has stated about the legacy of Canadian racism: "never mind academic Nazism in Germany in the 1930s — racism was quite respectable in Canadian universities in the same period." It was part of my own student experience in the 1950s. And as Howard Clarke, former President and Vice Chancellor at Dalhousie University, said in an almost confessional vein:

> The very old, but relatively small Black community in Nova Scotia has suffered overt discrimination over several centuries. The removal — or some would put it, the destruction — of Africville, the Black community on Bedford basin in the 1950's typifies their treatment.[31]

What of the 1907 bylaw in St. Croix Nova Scotia, used as recently as 1968 to prevent a three-year-old Black child from being buried in a cemetery with whites? What of the reported existence of three separate Canadian Klans as early as 1925? What of the Sir George Williams incident, and the protests around the killing of Michael Hadid, Albert Johnson, Buddy Evans, and more recently Wade Lawson, to name but a few? What of the talk of "differential treatment" in a study entitled *Perceptions of Discrimination Among Negroes And Japanese Canadians in Hamilton*, as early as 1944? Or of the existence of segregated schools in Ontario as late as 1965? Or reports of race riots at high schools in Cole Harbour and Digby Nova Scotia as recently as 1997 and 1998?[32]

Were these simply manifestations of unfounded Black Canadian paranoia, through the adoption of copycat political strategies? On this construction of Black Canada, reports of racial incidents are either anomalies, precipitated by "white fanatics," or the exaggerated stories of those who would view all negative incidences between Blacks and others as racist — those who would play the proverbial "race card." A similar form of this type of racist reasoning emerged around questions of Black immigrants from Jamaica in the summer of 1994. The debates focussed around the Just Desserts killing — Clinton Gayle's supposed wanton shooting of a Toronto police officer — form an ongoing part of a discussion of Blackness that revolves around immigration, criminality and racial activism. Versions of this debate can be traced at least as far back as the era of the underground railway and the Black Loyalists in Nova Scotia.

The dominant line of questioning in the Just Desserts incident was about whether Black immigrants, were deserving of Canadian citizenship; around issues of law and order. According to the implied logic, the young, Black, Jamaican immigrants involved in the shooting incidents simply had not overcome their "Jamaicaness," which consequently led them to criminal activity. Thus, a direct correlation is made between their "Jamaicanness" and their purported criminality, where Jamaica is construed as a site of Black criminality; and Canada as a site of "healthy, pluralist law and order." In the *Toronto Sun* on June 11, 1975, an article characterized Rastafarians as the most nefarious group of Jamaicans: "They [Jamaicans] will kill you for absolutely no reason.... This is what makes them so dangerous."[33] Implied is that those who have overcome their parochial "Jamaicanness" to become truly "Canadian" would not involve themselves in such un-Canadian activities.

Here, of course, we can see the binary relation that produces the marginal (Jamaican) as a consequence of the authority invested in the centre (Canadian). Canada is constructed as the ultimate site of pluralist rationality, while Jamaican is constructed as a synomyn for Black criminality. On this reasoning, to be "authentically" Canadian would be to shed the egregious (in this case Black) aspects of your particular cultural tradition (multiculturalism). Obversely, "Authentic Blackness" is linked to both irrational political activity and criminality reflecting the modern narrative. A direct correlation ismade between Black criminality and Black political activism; and between being a "good Canadian" and not being Black. For it may be that those same Black Jamaicans involved in criminal activity who are also involved in political activity. Here one can think of how the authorities hounded Dudley Laws; or the "strange" coincidence of media coverage of this Jamaican/Black law-and-order talk with discussions about the refashioning of immigration policy.

To paraphrase Paul Gilroy's claims about Black people in the British diaspora, Black people in the Canadian diaspora must refuse the binary of Black or Canadian "because [if] it remains the site of *constant contestation*, then the aim of the struggle must be to replace 'or' with the potential or possibility of an 'and.'"[34] As Austin Clarke has stated:

How do I resist the dermatology of Canadian culture imbued in me over all these years, and have the racial forwardness to regard myself as African? And why should I? Merely to give my protest a sharper context? Or more bluntly to evade the wounding of being called "nigger," "coloured," "Negro," "blasted Jamaican" or "West Indian"? Do I look more African than Canadian? If I permit this am I saying Canadians are white and Africans are Black. And if one is Black one cannot have been born here, one cannot be Canadian.[35]

The specific and diverse histories of the struggle of Black peoples in Canada, of Black Canadians — and here I am resisting the apolitical characterization of Black Canadians — from the pre-Confederation Black settlements in the Maritimes and Ontario, to the late twentieth-century migrations of Black peoples from Britain the Caribbean, and the African continent — cannot be denied. Black people in Canada, like elsewhere in the diaspora, have actively resisted their oppression; and there are long and diverse histories of Black political resistance in Canada.

Finally, I want to return to Orlando Patterson's discussion of Blacks "transcending particularistic cultures" and Nourbese Philip's statement about "cultural loss." Does not Patterson's idea of transcending our particularistic culture seem similar to certain dominant notions of Canadian identity, where Canada is seen as the site of transcendent pluralist politics (i.e., the Canadian vertical mosaic) or some version of the "just society?" I argue that part of the discussion of Blackness must involve an awareness of how caught up in modernity is the systematic use and abuse of Black bodies in the New World. The move beyond cultural "heritage," even given its pluralist twists, always seems to involve the systematic elision of the violence inherent in a univocal construction of Blackness. As Jacques Derrida has stated in another context:

Metaphysics — the white mythology which reassembles and reflects the culture of the West: the white man takes his own mythology, Indo-European mythology, his own logos, that is the mythos of his idiom, for the universal form of that he must still wish to call Reason... *erasing in the process that fabulous tyranny that produced, and continues to produce it* [my emphasis].[36]

Nourbese Philip's claim about "cultural loss" implies that there was or is an original, pure "Africanness," which, even if it cannot be accessed, informs our present viewpoints. But I argue that this "Africa" was itself always a site of political contestation, and that this supposedly lost African authenticity is inseparable from the politics of the construction of Africa and African identity that was on the way from the first colonial contact.

It is not that there are not analogies to be made across Black diasporic experiences, because there is a "transmigration of racial metaphors." However, in thinking of Blackness as diasporic, we must not erase the stubborn boundaries that "refuse to be erased."[37] Nourbese Philip herself acknowledges the existence of these boundaries when she characterizes the hiring of the African-American literary theorist Henry Louis Gates as an expert commentator by the Toronto producers of *Show Boat* as

> an essentially colonial approach to the debate: it implies that the United States and what happens there are the standard, that American responses ought to determine the reception of *Show Boat* in Canada.[38]

> [I]t is [therefore] to the diversity, not homogeneity, of Black experience that we must now give our undivided creative attention. This is not simply to appreciate the historical and experiential within and between communities, regions, country, and city, across national cultures, between diasporas, but also to recognize the other kind of difference that place, position, and locate Black people.[39]

Similarly, Austin Clarke has said of the May 4, 1992 Toronto Riot:

> It was not the first time that American racism had taken root in Canada in the minds of Black Canadians. It was not the first time that Black Canadians assumed an African brotherhood and sisterhood as the basis of their sympathy with their brothers across the border, negating any difference between American and Canadian racism.[40]

And yet

> the porter, on the train, the man in the washroom of the Towne

Cinema and the man who dared be a businessman have left their experiences... in the snow of this country.[41]

The representation of these experiences must speak of the diversity, plurivocality and heterogeneity of Black Canadian life — and here I am again emphasizing the political poignancy and pluriovocality of the sign "Black." Because "any ordinary day offers an opportunity to practice freedom, to create revolution internally, to rehearse for governance..."[42]

Endnotes

1. Cornel West, "Marxist Theory and the Specificities of African American Oppression," in *Marxism and the Interpretation of Culture.* Urbana and Chicago: University of Illnois Press, 1988.

2. Maya Angelou, *All God's Children Need Travelling Shoes*, (New York:Vintage Press, 1986), 96.

3. Stuart Hall, "What is the 'Black' in Black Popular Culture." *Black Popular Culture*, Gina Dent, (1992), 32.

4. "Racial tension is alive and well," *Toronto Telegram*, May 17, 1971.

5. Marlene Nourbese Philip, *Frontiers: Essays and Writings on Racism and Culture*, (Toronto:Mercury Press, 1992), 14

6. Orlando Patterson, "Towards a Future That Has No Past," Kirkland, ed., (1992), 136.

7. After Freud, we could not claim that repetition in this sense is possible, nor could we ever posit such a holistic reading of identity.

8. Stuart Hall, (see note 3), 28.

9. Ibid.

10. Paul Gilroy "Black Nationalism in the Sixties and the Nineties"

in *Black Popular Culture*, 302.

11. Stuart Hall (see note 3), 30.

12. It is important to note that for most of the great early modern thinkers, rational subjectivity did not include women. It is from within the parameters of claims about women's "natural" inability to be rational that the idea of not extending to women the right to universal suffrage was framed. John Stuart Mill is a notable exception to this rule See Mill J.S.,*The Subjection of Women*, (London: Virago, 1983).

13. It would go well beyond the purview of this chapter to examine the conjuncture between the modern construction of the self as a rational free agent, modern constructions of Black selves as irrational or "unrational not self," which must be stewarded into freedom, and modern exclusions of racial particularity as a defining category. But suffice it to say that the links go well into the heart of modernity. The question is whether modernity's commitment to principals of universality necessarily implies the exclusion of radicalized particularity.

14. This is what has been characterized as the "white man's burden," that is to civilize the "African savage" by stewarding her into modernity. Here it should also be noted that there is a direct correlation between hegemonic constructions of Africa and the African and that of women. See Edward Said, *Culture and Imperialism*, New York: Alfred A Knopf, 1994) p 218.

15. West, 23.

16. Hall, 26

17. West, 23

18. There seems to be some interesting conjunctures between what has come to be called the postmodern and discussions of post-coloniality, which go far beyond the purview of this paper. For an interesting exploration of this topic, see Stuart Hall's "When was the

Post-Colonial Thinking at the Limit," *The Post Colonial Question*, Iain Chambers and Lidia Curti, eds., (New York: Routledge, 1996).

19. Here it is worthy noting that for Jurgen Habermas the extension of the modernist ideal of rational subjectivity to those defined by early modern thinkers as intrinsically nonrational is part of a fulfilment of the project of modernity. See Jurgen Habermas, *The Philosophical Discourse of Modernity: Twelve Lectures*, (Cambridge: M.I.T. Press, 1997).

20. Chantal Mouffe, "Hegemony and New Political Subjects: Towards a New Concept of Democracy," in *Marxism and the Interpretation of Culture*, Cary Nelson and Lawrence Groosenberg, eds., (Urbana and Chicago: University of Illinois Press, 1988), 96.

21. Ibid.

22. Ibid.

23. Hall, 32.

24. Marlene Nourbese Philip *Frontiers: Essays and Writings on Racism and Culture*, (Toronto: Mercury Press, 1992), 196.

25. Hall p30.

26. As is generally the case with most theorizing in and around what has come to be called Black diasporic life, Paul Gilroy's recent work *Black Atlantic: Modernity and Double-Consciousness* completely ignores Canada as a site of Black diasporic life, only briefly mentioning it in relation to some comments by Donald Byrd, the jazz musician from Detroit, and to Martin Delany about Canada as representing freedom from slavery. See *Black Atlantic: Modernity and Double-Consciousness*, (Cambridge: Harvard University Press, 1993).

27. Here it must of course be noted that like the univocal construction of Blackness, univocal constructions of whiteness, in and of themselves elide the diversity and plurivocality of whites.

28. *Globe & Mail Magazine*, February 17, 1969, 30.

29. Kass Banning, "Rhetorical Remarks Towards The Politics of Otherness." *CineAction* (Spring 1989), 18.

30. *Globe & Mail Magazine*, 300.

31. Howard Clarke, *Proceedings National Symposium for University Presidents on Institutional Strategies for Race and Ethnic Relations in Canadian Universities*, (Kingston: Queen's University Pub., 1993), 8. It is interesting that several Black Nova Scotian writers and performance artists view the destruction of Africville and Seaview United Baptist Church as emblematic of the way Black folks are treated in Nova Scotia. See George Elliott Clarke, "Introduction," *Fire on the Water: An Anthology of Black Nova Scotian Writingm* Vol. 1, (Porters Lake: Pottersfield Press, 1991), 23.

32. See Anne Bains' "Fight at Auburn High," *This Magazine* July/August, 1997, 22-27.

33. *Toronto Star*, June 11, 1975, 20.

34. Hall, 30.

35. Clarke, 6.

36. Jacques Derrida, "White Mythology" in *Margins of Philosophy*, Alan Bass, tr., (Chicago: University of Chicago Press), 213.

37. Paul Gilroy, 305.

38. Marlene Nourbese Philip *Showing Grit:Showboating North of the 44th Parallel*, (Toronto: Poui Publications, 1993), 18.

39. Hall, 30.

40. Austin Clarke, "Public Enemies: Police Violence and Black Youth," *Point of View*, (Toronto: Harper Collins, 1992), 2.

41. Ibid.

42. Toni Cade Bambara, "Reading the Signs, Empowering the Eye: *Daughter of the Dust* and the Black Independent Cinema Movement," in *Black American Cinema*, Manthia Diawara, ed., (New York: Routledge, 1993), 126.

"Hey, ain't I Black too?":
The Politics of Becoming Black

Awad El Karim M. Ibrahim

Becoming cannot be a given, a mode of immediate being for being. [A] becoming is possible...only because on principle my being and my modes of being are heterogeneous. [And] being in becoming could be this synthesis only if it were so to itself in an act which would establish its own nothingness. If already I am no longer what I was, it is still necessary that I have to be so in the unity of a nihilating synthesis which I myself sustain in being; otherwise I would have no relation of any sort with what I am no longer, and my full positivity would be exclusive of the non-being essential to becoming (a rearranged text by Jean-Paul Sartre, 1980).

By Way of Becoming

The subject in progress (or process), *sujet en procès*, or becoming of being, or being as a continuous act of becoming is the central idea of this chapter. It is a Kristevan (1974; see also Nietzsche, 1977, p. 197) notion which assumes not fixity, but performativity (Butler, 1990); not being in thetic and static sense, but being as being which is never complete; and for this project, it assumes a being that is becoming Black. Based on a "critical ethnographic research project" (Ibrahim, 1998, 1999), which engages this notion as its backdrop, this paper will trace how a group of continental francophone African youths,[1] living in an metropolitan city in southwestern Ontario were in the process of becoming Blacks. This process was on the one hand marked by an *identification* with and a *desire* for North American Blackness; and it was, on the other, as much about gender and race as it was about language and cultural performance. I shall delineate these youths' desire for and identification with Blackness through language. They were learning Black English as a Second Language (BESL), which they accessed in and through Black popular culture, specifically rap music. Besides rap, they also took up and performed hip-hop cultural identity. My research is as much about my research "subjects," the youths, as it is about the present author. It is an ensemble of snapshots narrating how they and I were becoming Black.

The social categories of race and gender were central to this process of becoming Black. In the case of the African youths, for instance, although both young women and young men verbalized a strong identification with Blackness during interviews, the situation was different when it came to the intensity of bodily performance. Whereas all male students articulated and performed a strong identification with and a complete appropriation of hip-hop and rap through their dress, posture, walk, and talk, female students, depending on their age, tended to be more eclectic. The younger girls (twelve to fourteen years old) had the same linguistic and cultural practice and performance as the boys in their appropriation of rap and hip-hop, while the older girls tended to be more eclectic. For example, they combined hip-hop with "traditional" dress without any sense of contradiction. This noncontradictory combination of cultural practices, in the final analysis, became the law, the social order, which allowed students to form *their own* culture. The product of this combination is what I term, following Sartre (1980, p. 12) and Bhabha (1990), *the third space* (Ibrahim, 1998). Although I shall discuss it at length below, I will offer a preliminary definition here.

The third space is a product of *translating,* and in the process *negotiating,* two cultural norms and values. For example, immigrants, refugees, and otherwise displaced subjects who move from one geo-cultural and linguistic space to a new one are faced with the task of translating and hence understanding this new space. Analogically, but also literally, they become ethnographers. They observe how people in the new culture dress, walk, and talk; in short, they take note of who and how people *are* in the new culture. However, in the process, they translate not only the "new," but they also retranslate the "old" — the stored and already developed historical, cultural and linguistic memory from before emigration. The "old" and the "new" are then negotiated and combined, mostly unconsciously, to produce a cultural norm that is unique to the individual who goes through that experience. Henceforth, a third space is produced. This is the moment when two values, styles of dress, languages, and so on, are mixed together. This mixture, however, is not fixed, but performative: it is shifting, modified, and everchanging.

Borrowing from Judith Butler (1990), the idea of performativity is central to my research. Again, it is a concept which assumes not fixity but repetition, parody and continual acts of becoming. Following Simone de Beauvoir, Butler took gender or the category of woman as an example. (Note the synonymity between gender and race within Butler's conception.) She argues that one is not born a woman, one in fact becomes one. Therefore, gender for Butler is the repeated stylization of the body, a set of recurrent acts, words, gestures, or what Roland Barthes (1967/1983) calls complex semiological languages. These are signs that are open for signification and different readings since they cannot produce verbal utterances yet are ready to be spoken. For Butler, these complex languages are produced and performed on the surface of our bodies: in and through our modes of dress, walk, hairstyle, *maquillage*, lip gloss; and also in architecture, photographs, and so on.

I am contending, accordingly, that we perform our identities, desires, and investments, at least in part, in and through the complex semiological languages of our dress, walk and talk. This is what I have termed *ethnography of performance* (Ibrahim, 1998). As a research methodology, ethnography of performance also argues that the ethnographer's best access to the research subject's inner self is the subject's verbal and nonverbal performance. That is, the juxtaposition of what people actually and materially perform on and through their bodies with what they say and think about those performances combine to give ethnographers a more complete picture of their research subject's identity.

Performativity also assumes agency — the ground where questions of choice circulate, questions like: who do we as social subjects identify with?; who and what do we desire *to be*?; what choices do we make?; are they purely ours?; how do they come about?; what form do they take, and why? However, by now we know that "[t]he source of personal and political agency" — as Butler has convincingly noted — "comes not from within the individual, but in and through complex cultural exchanges among bodies in which identity itself is ever-shifting, indeed, where identity itself is constructed, disintegrated, and recirculated only within the context of a dynamic field of cultural relations" (1990, p. 127). To put it simply, our agency is governed, in the Foucauldian sense, by the socio-cultural context in which we live; which, in turn, governs our investments in who we want to be and what we want to become (1979). *Being* is distinguished here from *becoming*. The former is an accumulated memory, an understanding, a conception and an experience, upon which individuals interact with the world around them, whereas the latter is the process of building this memory of experience.

As a continental African, I was not considered Black in Africa: other terms served to patch together my identity, such as *tall*, *Sudanese*, and basketball player. However, as a refugee in North America, my perception of self was altered in direct response to the social processes of racism and the historical representation associated with Blackness — the previous signifiers became secondary to my Blackness — and I retranslated my being: I became Black. May 16, 1999 was a culminating date in my accumulative memory and experience of what it means *to be* Black (in Canada); it was the day I was officially declared Black. The following is an extract from my diary. At the time, I titled it *Being Under Surveillance: Who Controls My Black Body?* It is cited here to further our understanding of the everyday racism, human degradation, and general annihilation of Black people in North America. It is also a way of acknowledging how the present researcher is implicated in the research, and the questions I am asking.

> I know that experience can be a way to know and can inform how we know what we know. [And that] personal testimony…is such fertile ground for the production of liberatory [praxis] because it usually forms the base of our [knowledge and] theory making (bell hooks, 1994, p. 70).

Today was the last day of my trip to Toronto after a five-month absence in Ottawa. I had, to say the least, a wo(a)nderful time during my sojourn in Toronto: visited friends, had flavoury meals, and yes, saw *The Mummy*, too. It was 1:10 p.m. on a sunny and unexpectedly hot Sunday. I was more in the mood for poetry than for prose; and bicycling on St. George Street had never been as light. However, it is frightening how lightness can so easily whirl into an unbearable heaviness, and how heaviness can cause so much pain. It all began when I had just crossed the yellow light of Bloor Street West. I saw a white car curving into the bicycle lane and I heard hereafter a siren coming from it. Since I was bicycling, I was neither able to fully verify the car nor who was driving it nor why it was requesting me to stop. However, when it was fully halted before my bicycle, I realized it was a police car. From it came veering a rangy White man with full gear and a pair of sunglasses, along with a clean and handsome gun. My immediate thought was that it must be the bicycle helmet, since I was not wearing one; and seeing that there will always be a first time for our social experiences, I whispered to myself "oh God, this is my first ticket of my life." I was deadly mistaken.

He approached my bicycle and said "Have you ever being in trouble with the law before?" Shocked beyond any imaginable belief, I said "No." "Can I know why am I asked the question?"I added. "You fit the description of a man we are looking for, who just snatched a bag from Yorkville; and I just saw you around the Yorkville area," he said. Could I have avoided Yorkville, since to buy a muffler or a bandana in Yorkville one needs at least few hundred and I had only forty-two dollars in my pocket? Coincidences have their own logics, which are beyond my humble understanding. At this point, he began a walkie-talkie conversation with a dispatcher; and I realized when he said "I am talking to him right now" that it was the continuation of a previous dialogue. The phrase "I am talking to him right now" was, however, traumatic. Involuntarily, it triggered and brought alive my unforgettable political prison memory of the early 1990s, with the all-punishing dictatorial régime in Sudan. When memories are so deep, all they need is a match to find oneself burning and unwillingly shaking. The phrase was that match. It signified that I was already under surveillance; I was already "talked" about. Panopticism, somehow, keeps surfacing in my mind now. It was a situation where the marginalized and the invisible was becoming visible, if not the centre of surveillance; where the "fictions" I was immersed into came alive into "reality." Looking sternly into his eyes, I repeated "Can I know why I was stopped?" In a panoptic régime, I now understand, like all totalitarian régimes, the true opponent or enemy, if you like, is the person who asks questions. Squirmingly, his face turned red and he loudly regurgitated "I told YOU Sir that you fit the description of a man we are looking for."

Calmly but unaloofly, "And what is that description?", I wondered. "We are looking for a dark man with a dark bag," he said. First, I was curious about the "we." Who are "we?" I can hazard answers, but I am still not sure about the answer. Secondly I looked at my backbag which I was carrying, since I was leaving Toronto at 3 p.m., and it occurred to me that my bag was light blue with one very small black (or as he said "dark") stripe at the edge. More with my eyes than with my voice, I repeated after him "A DARK man?" Self-consciously, but pesteringly, he exclaimed "A Black man with a dark bag!" He insisted on my bag being "dark;" now I was significantly metamorphosed from "dark" into "black." Not that it matters either way, I reflected after, but it seems that some people can either not see or have "colour problem." "Do you live around here, Sir?" he asked. "I don't," I responded. Up until now, I have no idea why his eyes steered out and his face changed when I said I do not live in Toronto. "Where do you live, Sir?"; the appellation "Sir", at this point, was voiced with such an unease that I questioned the merit of its utterance. "Ottawa," I said. "What are you doing in Toronto?" What, indeed, are you doing in Toronto? I repeated to myself. Some questions, I guess, are meant to be repeated for their banality, if not stupefaction. I told him none of these; "I am visiting friends," I said. With an unconvinced face he murmured "Ohha!"

During this conversation, I saw another police car stopping behind the first; and from it came another White policeman. I was then asked for a piece of identification. I gave the first policeman my citizenship card. Before doing so, he asked me to lay down my (dark?) bag, which I did. With his order, I widely opened my bag for anyone in the street to see. Since it was a tourist area, with the well-attended Bata Shoe Museum, everyone was looking into my bag. Some, I observed, were pitying my plight and one White woman was smiling. I was not only pitying my situation, which was abstrusely absurd, I was pitying also that Toni Morrison's *Paradise*, Maragaret Atwood's *Alias Grace* and Julie Kristeva's *Reader* had to endure the same humiliation. These books were on top of my clothes. (Not that these books mattered in and for themselves, because they didn't. Disrespecfulness for the authors was what pestered me.) Anyway, it was getting closer to 2 p.m. and my ride for Ottawa was to leave at 3 p.m. At this point, I decided to use my University of Ottawa professor identification. I am still debating whether it was a favourable or unfavourable decision not to use it from the offset. After writing down my name and date of birth, he then announced to the dispatcher telling her "All is okay now."

With no apologies, I was ordered to collect my affairs and my bag and, as he uttered it, "You are free to go now." Given its inhumane nature, being under siege, believe me, is a feeling which should be avoided using all measures. Somehow, nonetheless, I pondered if the reasons for which I was stopped could or would be enough to stop any White man, should he be the suspect? Who among white men will be stopped? Most probably unsmartly dressed, with long bonny tail hair? Again, I kept wondering, what if I had not looked the policeman in the eyes and asked with a calm manner, which was not an evoked personae but a natural character, why I had been stopped? What if I was just a shy man who was genuinely frightened by the police? Given my panic, terror, and fright, what would have happened should I have ran? The wrath I had seen in that man's eyes, I would be ready to say, and it would certainly not be a hazard guessing given the historical relationship between the police and the Black body, was not reassuring.

I am also curious if my hip-hop dress, my emerging dreadlocks and my youthfulness did not form part of the reasons why I was stopped. To fathom answering these questions is irrelevant, but I can say the following to those (including an not-so-negligable number of my students) who address and think of racism as a problem that exists only south of the 49th parallel. First, to declare a problem, a reality, as nonexistent can only be a disavowal, a denial of its material existence, which certainly does nothing by way of finding an ultimate solution. Hence, it is significantly productive to admit that racism is rampant in our Canadian society, and denying its omnipresence does not help; and, second, no one should ever go through what I went through since it can only create distrust, melancholy and a lot of anger. Finally, at a recent French-language conference where I presented a paper, there was a professor who is the head of a very prestigious centre that deals with pedagogy (what an irony!) at the Universite of Laval. In subtle and convoluted philosophical terms, he questioned the merit of speaking about racism. Maybe waking up and smelling the coffee would not be such bad advice; and should he care to know: the coffee is no longer just French.

Nietzsche (1977) might have asked *"Muss es sein?"* ("Must it happen?"), and I might add: "Must it have happened?" As a response,

I here offer a theoretical proposition, which links my vignette with my research; it will also constitute a response to Nietzsche. It is a framework connected to the questions around the *gaze*: how am I perceived or imagined and what impact does this imaginary have on how I am gazed at, consumed, and related to? Even if — as Rousseau would have argued — we "live very much in the public gaze" (Taylor, 1994, p. 86), what nature does this "public gaze" have, and how much impact has it on our identities, identification, investments, and desires? Returning to the above incident: since it was written in my diary the wording might have been forcible, if not undiplomatic; but then writing as a healing does not require apologies. Also, the description of "everyday racism" (Essed, 1991) and discrimination might have been too diametrical; because we know that everyday racism is often too obscure to talk about, let alone tobe graphically detail. Moreover, you might already be wondering what all this has to do with the research I am about to present. Indeed, it has a lot to do with it: this is the very world in which my research subjects are socialized, inside and outside the school.

In what follows, I discuss first, my research, its contentions, propositions, and questions; and second, I introduce its methodology, site and subject. I then offer examples of African youths' speech in order to demonstrate the interplay between subject formation, identification and BESL learning. I also offer students' reflections and narratives on the impact of identification and becoming Black, and I conclude with remarks on the need to deconstruct this panoptic gaze, which limits, as we will see, African youths and my own life.[2]

This project constitutes part of the larger critical ethnographic research[3] I conducted at Marie-Victorin[4] (Ibrahim, 1998) between January and June 1996, which made use of my newly developed methodological approach, *ethnography of performance*. The research looks at the lives of a group of continental Francophone African youths and the formation of their social identity in an urban, French-language high school in southwestern Ontario. Besides their gendered and racialized experience, their youth and refugee status was vital to their *moments of identification*: that is, where and how they saw themselves reflected in the mirror of their society (cf. Bhabha, 1994). Put differently, once in North America, I contend, these youths were faced with a *social imaginary* (Anderson, 1983) in which they were already Blacks. This social imaginary was directly implicated in how and with whom they identified, which, in turn, influenced what and how they learned, linguistically and culturally. What they did learn is Black Stylized English (BSE), which they accessed in and through Black popular culture. They learned by taking up and repositing the rap linguistic and musical genre and, in different ways, acquiring and rearticulating the hip-hop cultural identity.

BSE is Black English (BE) with style; it is a subcategory. BE is what Smitherman refers to as *Black talk* (1994), which has its own grammar and syntax. BSE, on the other hand, refers to ways of speaking that do not depend on full mastery of the language. It banks more on ritual expressions, such as *whassup, whadap, whassup my Nigger*, and *yo, yo homeboy*, which are performed habitually and recurrently in rap. The rituals are more an expression of politics, moments of identification, and desire than they are of the dominant language — English — or of mastering the language per se. It is a way of saying, "I too am Black" or "I too desire and identify with Blackness."

By Black popular culture I mean films, newspapers, magazines, and more importantly, music, such as rap, reggae, pop, and rhythm and blues (R&B). The term *hip-hop* "is the overall naming apparatus" that "comprises everything from music to clothing choices, attitudes, language, and an approach to culture and cultural artifacts positing and collaging them in an unsentimental fashion" (Walcott, 1995, p. 5). More simply, I use hip-hop to describe a way of dressing, walking, and talking. The dress refers to the myriad shades and shapes of the latest *fly gear*: high-top sneakers, bicycle shorts, chunky jewelry, baggy pants, and polka-dotted tops (Rose, 1991, p. 227). The hairstyles, which include high-fade designs, dreadlocks, corkscrews, and braids are also part of this fashion. *The walk* usually means moving the fingers simultaneously with the head and the rest of the body while walking. *The talk*, however, is BSE. By patterning these behaviours, African youths enter the realm of becoming Black. As an identity configuration, the latter is deployed to talk about the *subject formation project* (i.e., the process and the space within which subjectivity is formed) that is produced in and by the process of language learning — in this case, learning BESL. More concretely, becoming Black meant learning BESL, as I will show below; yet the very process of BESL learning produced the epiphenomenon of becoming Black.

The central working tenet of my research was that, once in North

America, continental African youths enter a *social imaginary* (a discursive space or a representation) in which they are already constructed, imagined, and positioned — and thus treated by the hegemonic discourses and dominant groups — as Blacks. Here, I mean the white (racist) everyday communicative state of mind: "Oh, they all look like Blacks to me!" This positionality, which is offered to continental African youths through net-like praxis among exceedingly complex and mostly subconscious ways, does not acknowledge the differences in the students' ethnicities, languages, nationalities, and cultural identities. Fanon (1967, p. 116) sums up this net-like praxis brilliantly in writing about himself as a Black *Antillais* coming to Paris:

> I am given no chance, I am overdetermined from without. I am the slave not of the "idea" that others have of me but of my own appearance.... I *progress* [italics added] by crawling. And *already* [italics added] I am being dissected under white eyes, the only real eyes. I am *fixed*. Having adjusted their microtomes, they objectively cut away slices of my reality. I am laid bare... When people like me, they tell me it is in spite of my colour. When they dislike me, they point out that it is not because of my colour. Either way, I am locked into the infernal circle.

In other words, continental African youths[5] find themselves in a racially conscious society that, wittingly or unwittingly and through fused social mechanisms such as racist representations, asks them to fit racially somewhere. To fit somewhere signifies choosing or becoming aware of one's own being, which is partially reflected in one's language practice. Choosing, as we have already seen, however, is a question of agency, which is itself governed and disciplined by social conditions. For example, to be Black in a racially conscious society, like North American society, means that one is expected to be Black, act Black, and so be the marginalized *Other* (Hall, 1991; hooks, 1992). Under such disciplinary social conditions, continental African youths express their moments of identification in relation to African American and African Canadian cultures and languages, thus becoming Black. Taking up rap and hip-hop speaking are articulations of their desire to belong to a location, a politics, a memory, and a history.

The site of the research was a small Franco-Ontarian intermediate and high school (grades seven to thirteen), Marie-Victorin (MV). MV had an enrolment of approximately four hundred students from various ethnic, racial, cultural, religious, and linguistic backgrounds. Although it is a French-language school, students in the hallways predominately spoke English; Arabic, Somali, and Farsi were also common languages. The school had twenty-seven teachers, all of whom were white; and its archives show that up until the 1990s, students were also almost all white, except for a few students of African and Middle Eastern descent.

For over six months, I attended classes at MV, talked to students, and observed curricular and extracurricular activities two or three times per week. Because of my previous involvement in two-year long project at the same school I was well acquainted with MV and its population at the time of my research, especially its African students, with whom I feel I was able to develop a good communicative relationship.

Being the only Black adult — with the exception of one counsellor — and being myself a displaced subject, a refugee, and an African, had given me a certain familiarity with the students' experiences. I was able to connect with different age and gender groups through a range of activities, initially "hanging out"[6] with the students and later playing sports with various groups. I was also approached by these students for both guidance and academic help. Because of my deep involvement in the student culture, at times my status as researcher was forgotten, the line between the students and myself became blurred; and I believe that we shared a *safe space* of comfort that allowed us to open up, to speak and engage freely.

At the time of this research, students who were or had parents who were born outside Canada made up 70 percent of the school population at MV. Continental Africans constituted the majority within that percentage. This important African grou notwithstanding, the school continued to emphasize the theme of unity within this multicultural and multiethnoracial population. The slogan that the school advertised, for instance, was *unité dans la diversité* (unity in diversity). This discourse of unity, however, remained abstract and had little material bearing on the students' lives — the absence of people of colour among school personnel was a case in point. Rather, it was the Frenchness exhibited by many ethnic groups in the school that seemed to be the capital of its promotion. In fact, the French language, especially in Canada, represents a form of important *symbolic capital*, which, according to Bourdieu (1991), can be the key for accessing *material capital* — jobs, business, and so on. Hence, most African youths in fact come to Franco-Ontarian schools already possessing a highly valued symbolic capital because they speak *le français parisien* (Parisian French).

My research subjects formed part of a growing continental francophone African population in Franco-Ontarian schools, which I refer to as Black Franco-Ontarians. Their numbers have grown exponentially since the beginning of the 1990s. The participants varied, first, in terms of length of stay in Canada (from one to six years); second, in terms of their legal status (some were immigrants, but the majority were refugees); and, third, in terms of their gender, class, age, linguistic, and national background. They came from places as diverse as the Democratic Republic of Congo (formerly Zaïre), Djibouti, Gabon, Senegal, Somalia, South Africa, and Togo. With no exception, each of the African students in MV was at least trilingual, speaking English, French, and an African mother tongue, with varied histories of language learning and degrees of fluency in each language.

I spent the first month at MV hanging out with male and female African youths of different age groups, with their permission as well as their parents' and the school administration's permission. After a month, I chose ten boys and six girls for extensive ethnographic observation both inside and outside the classroom and the school and interviewed all sixteen of the youths. Of the ten boys, six were Somali speakers (from Somalia and Djibouti), one was Ethiopian, two were Senegalese, and one was from Togo. Their ages ranged from sixteen to twenty years. The six girls were all Somali speakers (also from Somalia and Djibouti), aged fourteen to eighteen years. The students chose the language in which their interview was conducted (English or French); and I translated the French-language interviews into English. The only Black counsellor and the former Black teacher were also interviewed.

Becoming Tri-or Multilingual: Sites and Sides of BESL Learning

Since these youths find themselves in a context where English is the medium of everyday interaction, they usually want to learn English rapidly. Elsewhere (Ibrahim, 1999), I have offered popular culture, especially television, as well as friendship and peer pressure as three mechanisms that hasten language acquisition. The African students felt particularly peer pressured in their early days at the school, when they were denigrated for not speaking English. Franco-Ontarian students, Heller has explained, use English in their everyday interaction, especially outside class (1994, 1992). If African students want to participate in school activities, they have no option but to learn English. Once it is learned, English becomes both a source of pride and a medium of communication, which allow African students to make friends and fully participate in North American public life.

Yet making friends, and even learning English, is influenced by the popular imaginary, the dominant source of representation: television. I asked each student "*Où est-ce que vous avez appris votre anglais?*" (Where did you learn English?). "*télévision*," they all responded. But I want to note that, within this *télévision* one particular representation — namely Black popular culture — seems to *interpellate*[7] (Althusseur, 1971) African youths' identity and identification. Because African youths at first have few African Canadian/American friends, they access their new Black cultural identities and Black linguistic practice through Black popular culture, especially rap music videos, television programs, and Black cinema. When I queried her about the most recent movies she had seen, Najat (14, F, Djibouti)[8] responded:

> I don't know, I saw *Waiting to Exhale* and I saw what else I saw, I saw *Swimmer*, and I saw *Jumanji*; so wicked, all the movies. I went to *Waiting to Exhale* wid my boyfriend and I was like 'men are rude' [laughs].
> Awad: Oh believe me I know I know.
> And den he [her boyfriend] was like "no women are rude." I was like we're like fighting you know and joking around. I was like, and de whole time like [laughs], and den when de woman burns the car, I was like "go girl!" You know and all the women are like "go girl!" you know? And den de men like khhh. I'm like "I'm gonna go get me a popcorn" [laughs]. (individual interview, English)

Besides showing the influence of Black English in the use of *de, den, dat*, and *wicked*, Najat's answer shows that youths bring agency and social subjectivities to the reading of a text. These subjectivities, importantly, are embedded in history, culture, and memory. The two performed subjectivities that interpellate in her Najat's reading of *Waiting to Exhale* were her race and gender: she identified with Blackness, as embodied in the female character; and with the Black/woman in burning her husband's car and clothes.

Another example (a videotaped moment) in a different context demonstrates the impact of Black popular culture on African students' lives and identities. Just before a focus group interview I had with the boys, *Electric Circus*, a local television music and dance program that plays mostly Black music (rap/hip-hop, reggae, soul and R&B) began. "*Silence!*" one boy exclaimed in French. The boys started to listen attentively to the music and watch the different fashions of the young people on the program. After the show, the boys' code switched between French, English, and Somali as they exchanged observations about the best music, the best dance, and the cutest girl. Rap and hip-hop and the corresponding dress were obviously at the top of their list.

These moments of identification point to the process of identity formation, which is, in turn, implicated in the linguistic norm to be internalized. The Western hegemonic representations of Blackness, Hall shows, are mostly negative and tend to work alongside historical and subconscious memories that facilitate interpretation by members of dominant groups (1990). Once African youths encounter these negative representations, they look for Black cultural and representational forms as sites for positive identification (Kelly, 1998). An important aspect of identification is that it works over a period of time and at the subconscious level. In the following excerpt, Omer (18, M, Ethiopia) addresses the myriad ways in which African youths are influenced by Black representations.

Black Canadian youths are influenced by the <u>Afro-Americans</u>. You watch for hours, you listen to Black music, you watch Black comedy, Master T.,[9] the *Rap City*, there you will see singers who dress in particular ways. You see, so. (individual interview, French)

Mukhi (19, M, Djibouti) explored identification by arguing that:

We identify ourselves more with the Blacks of America. But, this is normal, this is genetic. We can't, since we live in Canada, we can't identify ourselves with whites or country music you know [laughs]. We are going to identify ourselves on the contrary with people of our colour, who have our lifestyle you know. (group interview, French)

Mukhi evokes biology and genetic connection as a way of relating to Black. For Mukhi and all the students I spoke to, this identification is certainly connected to their inability to relate to dominant groups, the public spaces they occupied, and their cultural forms and norms. Alternatively, Black popular culture emerged for these youths as not only a site for identification, but also as a space for language learning.

"A'ait, Q7 in the House!"

Rap, for African students, was an influential site for language learning. However, the fact that rap was more prevalent in the boys' narratives than in the girls' raises the question of the role of gender in the process of identification and learning.

On many occasions, the boys performed typical gangster rap language and style, using linguistic as well as bodily performance, including name-calling. What follows are two of the many occasions on which students articulated their identification with Black America through the re/citation of rap linguistic styles.[10]

Sam: One two, one two, mic check. A'ait [alright], a'ait, a'ait.
Juma: This is the rapper, you know wha 'm meaning? You know wha 'm saying?
Sam: Mic mic mic; mic check. A'ait you wonna test it? Ah, I've the microphone you know; a'ait.
Sam: [laughs] I don't rap man, c'mon give me a break. [laughs] Yo! A'ait a'ait you know, we just about to finish de tape and all dat. Respect to my main man [pointing to me]. So, you know, you know wha 'm mean, 'm just represen'in Q7. One love to Q7 you know wha 'm mean and all my friends back to Q7... Stop the tapin' boy!
Jamal: Kim Juma, live! Put the lights on. Wordap. [Students talking in Somali] Peace out, wardap, where de book. Jamal 'am outta here.

Shapir: Yo, this is Shapir. I am trying to say peace to all my Niggers, all my bitches from a background that everybody in the house. So, yo, chill out and this is how we gonna kick it. Bye and with that pie. All right, peace yo.

Sam: A'ait this is Sam represen'in AQA [...] where it's born, represen'in you know wha 'm mean? I wonna say whassup to all my Niggers, you know, peace and one love. You know wha 'm mean, Q7 represen'in for ever. Peace! [Rap music]

Jamal: [as a DJ] Crank it man, coming up. [rap music] (group interview, English)

Of interest in these excerpts is the use of Black Stylized English, particularly the language of rap: "Respect for my main man," "represen'in Q7," "kick the free style," "peace out, wardap," "'am outta here," "I am trying to say peace to all my Niggers, all my bitches," "so, yo chill out and this is how we gonna kick it," "I wonna say whassup to all my Niggers," "peace and one love." Furthermore, when Shapir offers "peace to all" his "Niggers," all his "bitches," he is firstly reappropriating the word *Nigger*, an appellation common in rap/hip-hop culture. That is the case, although no friends, especially young people, commonly call a Black friend *Nigger* without its traditional racist connotation. Second, however, Shapir is using the sexist language that exists in rap (Rose, 1991). These forms of sexism have been challenged by female rappers like Queen Latifah and Salt 'n Pepa and were critiqued by fellow female and male students. For example, Samira (16, F, Djibouti) expressed her dismay at the sexist language found in some rap circles:

OK, hip-hop, yes I know that everyone likes hip-hop. They dress in a certain way, no? The songs go well. But, they are really really, they have expressions like fuck bitches, et cetera. Sorry, but there is representation. (group interview, French)

Here, Samira is addressing the impact that these expressions might have on the way society at large relates to and perceives the Black female body, which in turn influences how it is represented both inside and outside, rap/hip-hop culture. Hassan (17, M, Djibouti) also expressed his disapproval of this abusive language: "Occasionally, rap has an inappropriate language for the life in which we live, a world of violence and all that" (individual interview, French).

In rap style, one starts a performance by "checking the mic": "One two, one two, mic check." Then the rapper either recites an already composed lyric or otherwise "kicks a free style," displaying the spontaneity that characterizes rap. The rapper begins the public performance by introducing herself or himself with a true or made-up name — "Yo this is Shapir" — and thanks her or his "main man," or best friend, who often introduces the rapper to the public. Specific to gangster rap, one represents not only oneself but a web of geophysical and metaphorical spaces and collectivities that are demarcated by people and terratorial spaces: "Represen'in Q7," "a'ait, this is Sam represen'in AQA." At the end of the performance, when the recitation or freestyle is completed, again one thanks the "main man" and "gives peace out" or "shad out" (shout out) to the people.

The boys were clearly influenced by rap lyrics, syntax and morphology (in their broader semiological sense), especially by gangster rap. Depending on their age, the girls, on the other hand, had an ambivalent relationship to rap; although both boys and girls used the same three strategies in learning ESL in general and BSE in particular through music: listening, reading and reciting. For instance, Jamal was listening to the tunes and lyrics while reading and following a written text. Acting as a DJ, he then repeated not only the performer's words and expressions but also practiced his accent.

On their part, the girls used similar strategies to Jamal's. For example, during a picnic organized by a mixed group of students, the girls listened to music while following the written text and reciting it (complete with accents) along with the singer. The girls' choice of music (including Whitney Houston and Toni Braxton) differed in that it was softer than that chosen by the boys and contained mostly romantic themes.

For the most part, the older girls/women (sixteen to eighteen years old) tended to be more eclectic in how they related to hip-hop and rap. Their eclecticism was evident in how they dressed and in what language they learned. Their dress was any combination of elegant middle class, partially hip-hop, and traditional, and their learned language was what Nourbese Philip (1991) calls *plain Canadian English*. The younger girls (twelve to fourteen years), on the other hand, like the boys, dressed in hip-hop style and performed BSE.

In spite of their ambivalent relationship to rap and hip-hop, I detected the following three features of Black English in both the older and the younger girls' speech: 1) the absence of the auxiliary *be* (e.g., "they so cool," "I just laughing" as opposed to *they are so cool* and *I am just laughing*); 2) BE negative concord (e.g., "all he [the teacher] cares about is his daughter you know. If somebody just dies or if I decide to shoot somebody you know, he is *not* doing *nothing* [italics added]"; and 3) the distributive *be* (4 occasions, e.g., "I be saying dis dat you know?" or "He be like 'Oh, elle va être bien' [she's going to be fine]"). These BE markers are expressions of the influence of Black talk on the girls' speech and performances of the girls' identity location and desire, which they apparently ally with Blackness.

Performing Acts of Desire

I have identified rap and hip-hop as influential sites in African students' processes of becoming Black, which in turn affected what and how they learned. Their narratives also show that the youths were quite cognizant of their identification with Blackness and the impact of race on their choices. In the following conversation, Mukhi reflects on the impact of rap (as just one among many Black popular cultural forms) on his life and others' lives around him:

> Awad: But do you listen to rap for example? I noticed that there are a number of students who listen to rap eh? Is …
> Sam: It is not just us who listen to rap, everybody listens to rap. It is new.
> Awad: But do you think that that influences how you speak, how…
> Mukhi: *How we dress, how we speak, how we behave* [italics added]. (group interview, English)

These linguistic patterns and dress codes that Mukhi addresses are accessed and learned by African youths through Black popular culture. As I already noted, these patterns do not require or concern mastery and fluency, instead, they are performative acts of desire and identification. Amani (16, F, Somalia) contends that:

> We have to wonder why we try to really follow the model of the Americans who are Blacks? Because *when you search for yourself, search for identification, you search for someone who*

reflects you, with whom you have something in common [italics added]. (group interview, French)

Hassan supported Amani as follows:

> Hassan: Yes yes, African students are influenced by rap and hip-hop because they want to, yes, they are influenced probably a bit more because it is the desire to belong maybe.
> Awad: Belong to what?
> Hassan: To a group, belong to a society, to have a model/fashion [he used the term *un modèle*]; you know, the desire to mark oneself, the desire to make, how do I say it? To be part of a <u>rap</u> society, you see. It is like getting into <u>rock and roll</u> or <u>heavy metal</u>. (individual interview, French)

Hence, one invests where one sees oneself mirrored. Such an investment includes linguistic as well as cultural behavioural patterns. In an individual interview, Hassan told me it would be unrealistic to expect to see Blackness allied with rock and roll or heavy metal, as they are socially constructed as white music. Similarly, he argued emphatically that African youths would had every reason to invest in basketball — constructed as a Black sport — but not hockey, for example.

Towards a Pedagogy of the Imaginary

> When it encounters resistance from the other, self-consciousness undergoes the experience of desire — the first milestone on the road that leads to the dignity of the spirit... As soon as I desire I am asking to be considered. I am not merely here-and-now, sealed into thingness. I am for somewhere else and for something else. I demand that notice be taken of my negating activity insofar as I... do battle for the creation of a human world — that is, of a world of reciprocal recognition (Fanon, 1967, p. 218).

The desire on the part of African youths, particularly the boys, to invest in basketball is analogous to their desire to learn BESL. Learning is hence neither aimless nor neutral, nor is it without the politics of identity. As I have shown, a second-language learner can have a marginalized linguistic norm as a target, depending on who is learning what, why and how. I have also discussed how these youths were becoming Blacks, which meant learning BESL. Becoming Black, I have argued, was an identity signifier produced by and producing the very process of BESL. To become Black is to become an ethnographer who translates and looks around in an effort to understand what it means to be Black in Canada, for example. In becoming Black, the African youths were interpellated by Black popular cultural forms, rap and hip-hop, as sites of identification. Gender, however, was as important as race in determining what was being chosen and translated.

Choosing the margin, then, is simultaneously an act of investment, an expression of desire, and a deliberate counterhegemonic undertaking. Choosing rap must be read as a special act of resistance. Historically, rap was formed as a voice for voicelessness and performed as a prophetic language that addresses silence, the silenced, and the state of being silenced. It explores the hopes and the political, historical, and cultural experience of the *Black Atlantic* (Gilroy, 1993). As Jamal argued,

Black Americans created rap to express themselves; how do I say it? Their ideas, their problems, [and] if we could integrate ourselves into it, it is because rappers speak about or they have the same problems we have. (individual interview, French)

Such problems may include human degradation, police brutality, and everyday racisms (Essed, 1991; Anthias and Yuval-Davis, 1992). I introduced my incident with the police in order to explore the socio-political context where African youths and I circulate and form our identities, as well as to show everyday racisms, human degradation, and the impact of being under the hegemonic gaze.

Of course, the gaze is invisible, as we know, which renders any attempt to address it or deconstruct it even more formidable. Nonetheless, I would like to undertake such a task by proposing what I want to term a *pedagogy of the imaginary*: a critical pedagogy that aims to deessentialize and decolonize public spaces, both represented and imagined. It poses the following questions: how do we as a nation, groups, and individuals imagine ourselves as well as others; what impact does it have on others, and how can we as pedagogues work with this imaginary to make people imagine themselves and others differently?

The African students (and I), it seems to me, were casualties of fixity. That is, they/we were already fixed in an identity, already slotted in an imaginary, which in complex ways limited how and where they/we circulated their/our identities. A (fixed) identity is not based on who one *is*: one's own social-cultural, national, and linguistic identity. It is based, on the contrary, primarily on how one appears, one's racial identity: "Oh, they all look like Blacks to me!" This state of mind is thus largely dependent on already circulating hegemonic and historical discourses and representations of Blackness. Hence, such fixed identities do no heed how one sounds when speaking to a subject; all they require is a look, a set of clothes, an attitude, and so on.

It is this imposed fixity that we need to further reckon with. For now, I want to argue that it is an act of symbolic violence that requires no intentionality. Intentionally or not, symbolic violence had been exerted on African students by denying them their full identities, which encompassed more than their racial identity. Put differently, African students appeared to have fallen prey to this fixity, which imposed on them the already established North American order, discourses, and historical representations of Blackness. What we visibly "see" can be deceiving; and although we may all project preconceived identities on others in one way or another in our everyday interactions, when this imposition is coupled with power, its consequences can be traumatic, as evidenced by my incident with the police.

The pedagogy of the imaginary addresses those who can maneuver those socio-histoical structures that allow them to exert such violence.[11] Paulo Freire has called them the oppressors (1993); those who possess the power to represent, structure and restructure nations and narrations, and thus write and rewrite.

In formulating a pedagogy, we need to imagine race as well as gender, as categories of visible subjects, which occupy sites that are recognizable only through an actual, ethnographic, and *material encounter* and not an imagined one. In such sites, Blackness may refer to a gay, middle class, writer, university professor subject; and gender may refer to a lesbian, upper middle class, company executive subject, and so on. In other words, we need to imagine subject categories as always occupying different and multiple sites, albeit perhaps not in abundant numbers in some sites. Since the public imaginary has historically been colonized by a self-serving power bloc, representing only their own kind, these categories have rarely been represented or discussed as ever-changing.

The pedagogy of the imaginary in this context, then, is a hopeful yet critical pedagogy that "allows us to affirm multiple Black identities, varied Black experience. It also challenges colonial imperialist paradigms of Black identity, which represent Blackness one-dimensionally in ways that reinforce and sustain white supremacy" (hooks, 1990, p. 28). It is a pedagogy which eventually help us imagine, in the case of African students, for example, that Blackness has cultural, national, religious, and linguistic repertoires that differ from those evident in North American Blackness. Blackness is *de facto* multicultural, multilingual, and multiethnic.

Within this pedagogy, the *encounter* is of a particular significance in rupturing the normalizing gaze. Here, I am emphasizing symbolic encounters, where texts and representations become vitally important. Specifically, I am proposing rap, hip-hop, and Black popular culture in general as pedagogical moments, "sites of encounter," if you like, with Blackness in the classroom. In so doing, I am pointing to the horizon of possibilities of using Black cultural productions, particularly musical, literary, and cinematic representations as moments of rupture of what hooks has called "colonial imperialist paradigms" where Black identities are represented "one-dimensionally." As we have seen, Black popular culture (rap and hip-hop in particular) are curriculum sites where learning takes place and identities are invested.

In the language of antiracism education (Dei, 1996; James, 1995), proposing Black popular culture as a curriculum site is, on the one hand, a call to centralize and engage marginalized subjects, their voices, and their ways of being and learning. On the other hand it is to revisit this question: in the case of African students, whose language and identity are we as pedagogues teaching and assuming in the classroom if we do not engage rap or hip-hop? This proposition then, entails a legitimization of a form of knowledge otherwise perceived as illegitimate (Ibrahim, 1999).

The encounter with Black cultural forms, moreover, is and must be seen as a moment of critical examination instead of passive consumption. Because Black popular cultural forms are also social and historical productions, they are as much sites of hope as they are sites of critique. Rap and hip-hop, as noted, are not exceptions to dominant discourses of sexism and homophobia (see Rose, 1991; Walcott, 1995). They should therefore not be readily consumed but critically framed, studied, and engaged with (Ibrahim, 1999). Yet, rap and hip-hop are also sites of hope, a hope that will eventually broaden the horizon of possibility (Simon, 1992); the possibility that Blackness is seen and imagined for what it is: multiple, complex, and multilayered. A hope that would allow all students, but particularly those from dominant groups, to be able to "see" multiple ways of speaking, being, and learning. In Paulo Freire's (1993) language, introducing rap and hip-hop in class, especially in the case of African students, is to hope to link their world, identities, desires, and investments with their words.

Works Cited

Althusser, L. (1971). *Lenin and Philosophy*. London: New Left Books.

Anderson, B. (1983). *Imagined Communities: Reflections on the Origin and Spread of Nationalism*. London: Verso.

Anthias, F. and Yuval-Davis, N. (1992). *Racialized Boundaries*. London and New York: Routledge.

Barthes, R. (1983). *Elements of Semiology*. New York: Hill and Wang. (Original work published 1967)

Bhabha, H. (1994). *The Location of Culture*. London and New York: Routledge.

Bourdieu, P. (1991). *Language and Symbolic Power*. (G. Raymond and M. Adamson, Trans.). London: Polity Press.

Butler, J. (1990). *Gender Trouble: Feminism and the Subversion of Identity*. New York: Routledge.

Dei, G.J.S. (1996). *Anti-racism Education: Theory and Practice*. Halifax: Fernwood Publishing.

Essed, P. (1991). *Understanding Everyday Racism*. Sage Publications.

Fanon, F. (1967). *Black Skin White Masks*. New York: Grove Weidenfeld.

Foucault, M. (1979). *Discipline and Punish: The Birth of the Prison* (A. Sheridan, Trans.). New York: Vintage Books.

Freire, P. (1993). *Pedagogy of the Oppressed*. New York: Coninuum.

Gilroy, P. (1993). *The Black Atlantic: Modernity and Double*

Consciousness. London & New York: Routledge.

Hall, S. (1991). Ethnicity: Identity and Difference. *Radical America*, 13 (4), 9-20.

Hall, S. (1990). Cultural Identity and Diaspora. In J. Rutherford (Ed.) *Identity, Community, Culture, Difference* (pp. 222-237). London: Lawrence & Wishart.

Heller, M. (1994). *Crosswords: Language, Education and Ethnicity in French Ontario*. Berlin and NY: Mouton de Gruyter.

Heller, M. (1992). The Politics of Codeswitching and Language Choice. *Journal of Multilingual and Multicultural Development* Vol. 13: 1&2: 123-142.

hooks, bell (1994). *Teaching to Transgress: Education as the Practice of Freedom*. London & New York: Routledge.

hooks, bell (1992). *Black Looks*. Boston, MA: South End Press.

hooks, bell (1990). *Yearning: Race, Gender, and Cultural Politics*. Toronto: Between the Lines.

Ibrahim, A. (1999). Becoming Black: Rap and Hip-Hop, Race, Gender, Identity, and the Politics of ESL Learning. *TESOL Quarterly*, Vol. 33, No.3, 349-369.

Ibrahim, A. (1998). *'Hey, whassup homeboy?' Becoming Black: Race, Language, Culture, and the Politics of Identity. African Students in a Franco-Ontarian High School*. Unpublished doctoral dissertation, OISE: University of Toronto.

James, C. E. (1995). Multiculturalism and Antiracism Education in the Canadian Context. *Race, Gender and Class*, 2 (3), 31-48.

Kelly, J. (1998). *Under the Gaze: Learning to Be Black in White Society*. Halifax: Fernwood Publishing.

Kristeva, J. (1974). *La Révolution du Langage Poétique* [Revolution in Poetic Language] Lautréament et Mallarmé.

Nietzsche, F. (1977). *A Nietzsche Reader*. New York: Penguin Classics.

Philip, M.N. (1991). *Harriet's Daughter*. Toronto: The Women's Press.

Ogbu, J. and Fordham, S. (1986). Black Students' School Success: Coping with the 'Burden of Acting White'. *The Urban Review*, Vol. 18, No. 3, 176-206.

Rose, T. (1991). "Fear of a Black Planet": Rap Music and Black Cultural Politics in the 1990. *Journal of Negro Education*, Vol. 60, No.3: 276-290.

Said, E. W. (1994). *Culture and Imperialism*. New York: Alfred A. Knopf.

Sartre, J.-P. (1980). *Being and Nothingness: A Phenomenological Essay on Ontology.* (Hazel E. Barnes, Trans.). New York: Pocket Books.

Simon, R. I. (1992). *Teaching Against the Grain.* New York: Bergin and Garvey.

Simon, R. I. and Dippo, D. (1986). On Critical Ethnography Work. *Anthropology & Education Quarterly,* Vol. 17: 195-202.

Smitherman, G. (1994). *Black Talk: Words and Phrases from the Hood to the Amen Corner.* Boston: Houghton Mifflin.

Taylor, C. (1994). The Politics of Recognition. In D. T. Goldberg (ed.) *Multiculturalism: A Critical Reader.* Oxford: Blackwell.

Walcott, R. (1995). *Performing the Postmodern: Black Atlantic Rap and Identity in North America.* Unpublished doctoral dissertation, OISE: University of Toronto.

Endnotes

1. Given their arbitrary natures as a social construction, I use *youths* interchangeably with *students, boys,* and *girls.* By *continental African,* I mean Africans from the continent Africa, as opposed to *diasporic African* (e.g., African Canadians or African Americans).

2. The following section is a revised version excerpt Ibrahim, 1999.

3. For Simon and Dippo (1986, p. 195), *critical ethnographic research* is a set of activities situated within a project that works its way towards social transformation. This project is political as well as pedagogical, and the researcher's identity and his or her racial, gender, and class embodiments necessarily govern the research questions and findings. The project, then, according to Simon and Dippo, is "an activity determined both by real and present conditions, *and* certain conditions still to come which it is trying to bring into being" (p. 196). The assumption underpinning my project is the idea that Canadian society is "inequitably structured and dominated by a hegemonic culture that suppresses a consideration and understanding of why things are the way they are and what must be done for things to be otherwise" (p. 196).

4. All names are pseudonymous.

5. Based on my incident with the police, I would also include myself here, hence would respond positively to Nietszche's *"Muss es sein?"*

6. Staying somewhere to familiarize oneself with the place, its people, and their ways of '"being" in that space. In the school, these sites are informal, such as hallways, the schoolyard, the school steps, the cafeteria, and the gymnasium, where the people are comfortable enough to speak their minds.

7. The subconscious ways in which individuals, given their genealogical history and memory, identify with particular discursive spaces and representations and the way this identification participates thereafter in the social formation of the Subject.

8. Each student name is followed by age, gender (F=Female, M=Male), and country of origin; and each extract is followed by the type of interview (individual or group) and the language in which it was conducted. The following transcription conventions are used: underlined text English spoken within French speech or French spoken within English speech

9. Master T. is an MC of a local Canadian rap music TV program called *Rap City* which airs mostly American rap lyrics.

10. The names cited in the extracts are Sam (19, M, Djibouti), Juma (19, M, Senegal), Jamal (18, M, Djibouti), and Shapir (17, M, Somalia).

11. Although my primary targets are those in positions of power, I do, in fact, address everyone. I am including Black peoples here; and this may solve the phenomenon of "acting white" (Ogbu and Fordham, 1986), at least in part. That is, if Black peoples can negotiate the fact that, given the multiplicity of social and class location that Blackness may occupy, what belongs to Whites may as well belong to Blacks and vice versa. If they can expect, imagine, and therefore feel that, as C. L. R. James used to say, Beethoven belongs as much to Blacks and West Indians as he does to Germans (see Said, 1994), they must see that academic success is as much a Black phenomenon as it is a White phenomenon.

The Politics of Essentialism:
Rethinking "Black Community"

Renuka Sooknanan

Show Boat: "Staging" Canadian Blackness

The controversy that surrounded the 1993 stage production of *Show Boat* in Toronto was as much a commentary on community as it was on race, racism, stereotyping (negative imagery and characterization that portrayed Blacks as shiftless or noble savages), the pervasiveness of racist mythologies, racist language, and misrepresentations.[1] As a result of a proliferation and dissemination of information in the form of dialogue, meetings, protests, media attention (from local so-called ethnic newspapers to mainstream television programs), and activist work, the term "Black community" received a great deal of play; focussing on the issues of race and racism, "Black community" remained an accepted, unchallenged category — an essential category — understood to stand in for Black Canadians mapping the national landscape. Not only was *Show Boat* being "staged," but so was a particular closed version of Black community — a closed performance of Canadian Blackness.

While the very question of community was sidelined during the *Show Boat* struggle, a central concern was with anti-racism action. The range of perspectives, from the most conservative to the most radical (Anti-Racist Action's work, for example), represented a dialogic exercise about racism in Canada. Because issues of racism and marginalia have never been sufficiently dealt with in Canada, controversies like the *Show Boat* production continually throw up a disquieting return of the repressed. Blackness in Canada is a kind of ongoing erasure, an invisible visibility repressed in the psyche of a nation flogging a failed multiculture. It is in the face of such a constant disposability, continued abuse and visited violence that

Black community takes shape.[2] There is an overall present immediacy and urgency to the situation. I'm suggesting that community of this kind is a critical response to an everyday shared language and culture in which racism's currency is formidable, aggressive — and symptomatic of a nation's desire to remain locked into two so-called "founding races."

So while a critical response is a necessary survival strategy for the Black community as a way of addressing oppression and discrimination, it is important to note that the questions I'm posing here seek a detailing of Black community such that the very meaning of Blackness, that which qualifies as Blackness, as Black community, is up for investigation as a category. In many ways, "qualification" is what is at stake: what is imagined when Black community is spoken, made recognizable as something that has unsurmountable wholeness and oneness? An additional question asks: upon what basis is identification made thinkable, knowable enough to be easily translated and agreed upon to mark a unified perfomance? Moreover, I'm interested in figuring how identity at the time of *Show Boat*, was an already "staged" act. I'm playing with the idea of "stage" and "performance" in their doubleness, as well as shaking down the very binary of inside/outside which always attempts to construct community as conversant with the project of mimesis.

Show Boat demonstrated that there was an already familiar es-*sense* at work in order for Black community to organize against the show; how we want to understand this is not a matter of choice, however, not when what is circulated about Blackness is a stable and recognizable referential. I don't believe that this kind of demonstration, which relies on simple or authentic versions of Black community, is a critical way of understanding community — specifically, Black community. I argue that such a constitution of Black community does not exist. Black community is not a static category: it is complex and diverse. The complexity and changeability of Black community is a kind of performing of Blackness that problematizes nostalgic nuances and the desire for a community of sameness. Mine is a refusal to think Black communtiy as anything but complex, ethical, political, because it is in the making and unmaking of Black community as a *process* that Black community gains its variability, its complex meaning, its *politics* — *this*, I believe, is "a grammar for Black."

A Question of "the" Black Community

I would venture so far as to say that there is no such thing as *the* Black community. I would further argue that "*the* Black community" is a nebulous sign, which doesn't allow for complexity. It encompasses a stasis appeal and closures which, as a stable sign, makes thinking Black community an impossibility. What is *the* Black community? I raise the question for many reasons — mostly for conceptual clarity — but also to disrupt the very workability of the idea of essence in thinking community and Blackness. The *Show Boat* production might have been an ideal moment in the construction of Black Canada to invent a cosmologic interiority of Black community as complexly and contingently figured. Such an opportunity evaded the ongoing organizing at the time, I believe, because the issues taken up around the *Show Boat* were set apart from revisioning exercises around community. Instead, what became visible throughout the struggle was public outrage at problems such as racist imagery, language, and so on. While these are important concerns of any discussion on racism and representation, what needs to be clarified is the fact that this anti-racist moment could have devised a criticality about Black community. There have been other recent historical events, such as the *Into the Heart of Africa* exhibit at the Royal Ontario Museum and The Barnes Collection, where a dialogue on Black community was not taken up with any urgency. Pockets of racist incidents are not nearly enough though to formulate complicated identificatory schemes for thinking Black Canada or Black community. It is time to provoke a conversation.

When Stuart Hall problematized the "Black" in Black popular culture,[3] he called for the "end of the innocence of the Black subject," or, rather, "the end of the innocent notion of an essential Black subject."[4] Hall's gesture provokes us to move beyond conceptualizations of settled, stable categories. To destabilize by contesting the familiarity and certainty that reside within the frames of "Black" and of "Black community" is, in part, the task of the end of the innocence. And Hall reminds us that unsettling the terrain in the project of "innocence" is not an end in itself, but a beginning gesture, signalling the work ahead as cultural workers, activists, academics and others, to deploy a cacophony of discourses on how Blackness — and by extension, Black community — can be imagined.

While it may seem that this paper is thinking two categories of analysis, Black and community, what is important to understanding these categories is the dynamic that involves theorizing them both. De-essentializing "Black" will help us think about how community has similarily been treated as something knowable and definitive. At issue is how shifts in meaning making make it possible to move from moments of categorical stabilization to the plurality of possible meanings. The end of the innocence is an invitation, or quite possibly a demand, to think multiplicity and to rethink how hegemonic, homogenous categories have come to stand in for the various representations that are repressed under the signs of Black and of Black community.

When I speak of plurality of meaning or of multiplicity I'm moving from the place of stable knowing to unmarked cartographies of continuous shifts. Such conceptual destabilizing rejects unity and oneness, a move that ultimately makes what is knowable chaotic. Emptying identificatory categories, sifting away and decentring subject positions, is aimed at fashioning the contingent character of identity struggles. So meaning making is what's up for grabs in the performativity of Blackness. By performativity I mean the various ways in which communities create and recreate themselves; [5] it is the communicative and expressive possibilities produced through particular performed strategies (through popular music, local resistance, literature, orality, memory, coalitions, wardrobe stylings, the politics of hair, et cetera) that enable the survival of communities. Performance in this sense always infers and refers to a reinvention, a certain interpretation that aids in furthering the idea of change and shift and which, at its very core, demonstrates disruptive and transgressive signifying practices. This notion of performance and creativity is vitally important when we consider the following opposite poles: essence and anti-essence (we can also say, the authentic vs. variability). Changeability and shifting are part of the ongoing problematic of articulating difference and identity. When the idea of performance is invoked I want to be clear that the shifts and changes I refer to occur at the level of meaning making. Performance entails communication through (between, within) various strategies of articulation at its limits. Performativity is always an "outside" styling/fashioning: it signals the place of translation, hybridity, and intertextual borrowings, adapted by singularity.

I want to add that this call for a rethinking of Black community is not an easy matter. The difficulty lies in the fact that certain risks need to be taken in order to address Blackness in Canada. Opening up a discussion on shifting meaning so that Black community resists any attempt to nostagically define itself is part of that risk. I hope it is a dialogue that will provoke intense moments of clarity and visioning. Mostly, I'm thinking of this task as a further move in the war of manoeuvers, the play of identifications and a respect to the processes inherent in making difference count. I want to discourage any celebratory definitions of Black community that locate Blackness within multicultural and race relations strategies; these, I think, will limit the possibilities of becoming community and of becoming Black.

Thinking Through the Politics of Essentialism

How do we begin to peel away the fundamental and commonsensical idea of Black community? One important methodological arguement is that the connection between the way common sense and essence work. Several years ago, Eroll Lawrence took up the Gramscian notion of common sense and refined it to think about issues of race and racism in Britain.[6] For Lawrence, the currency of common sense ideology lies in the practical sensibility of the everyday. I am interested in the application of Lawrence's formulaic understanding of common sense in order to script a reading of the commonsensical that makes questions of Black community thinkable in the everyday. Lawrence maintains that common sense is usually used to denote a down-to-earth "good sense." He explains:

> [i]t is thought to represent the distilled truths of centuries of practical experience: so much so that to say of an idea or practice that it is only common sense, is to appeal over the logic and argumentation of all intellectuals to what all reasonable people know in their "hearts of hearts" to be right and proper. Such an appeal can act at one and the same time to foreclose any discussion about certain ideas and practices and to legitimate them.[7]

Lawrence's conceptual reconfiguration suggests that common sense is a certain appeal couched in a particular knowledge that acts to foreclose. It is this combination of appeal, knowledge and foreclosure that is definitive in the relationship between Black community and essence. Yet it is also the connection between knowledge and "right and proper" that is interesting in this quote. Knowledge is being understood by Lawrence in an everyday way; "right and proper," as associated with this everyday sensibility, has a particular staying quality, a feeling of a deep and profound knowing. The utterance "hearts of hearts," also suggests that our knowing is grounded in that everyday context: it is the philosophy of the everyday, which is shared by everyday folk. Lawrence goes on to argue that:

> [t]he contradictory nature of common sense means that it should not be thought of as constituting a unified body of knowledge. It does not have *a* theory underlying or "hidden beneath" it, but is perhaps best seen as a "storehouse of knowledges" which has been gathered together, historically, through struggle.[8]

The contradiction is clear. How can we understand some form of knowing, from our "hearts of hearts" without this "knowing" constituting a unified body of knowledge?

In fact, Chris Weedon has argued that common sense indeed has a contradictory quality to it. She maintains that "common sense knowledge is not a monolithic, fixed body of knowledge. It is often contradictory and subject to change... Its political effects depend on the particular context in which it is articulated."[9] In spite of this contradiction, Weedon notes that the power of commonsensical knowledge "comes from its claim to be natural, obvious and therefore true. It looks to 'human nature' to guarantee its version of reality. It is the medium through which already fixed 'truths' about the world, society and individuals are expressed."[10] So, more than a "storehouse" of knowledge, common sense is a medium. But again, like in Lawrence's formulation, Weedon's exploration of common sense acknowledges the idea of the "natural" in its definition. The importance of Weedon's interpretation, nonetheless, is clear when she states "truths" (and therefore, meaning) are first fixed and then worked through the idea of common sense in order to be delivered, understood, and made thinkable in the everyday. Weedon suggests that "these supposed truths are often rhetorically reinforced by expressions such as 'it is well known that,' 'we all know that' and 'everybody knows' which emphasize their obviousness and put social pressure on individuals to accept them." [11] Like Lawrence, Weedon's definition also registers the contradictory meaning of common sense.

For both Lawrence and Weedon, common sense has a certain "natural" quality, which gives it meaning and sustainability. However, "natural" has an insidious flavour when it comes to addressing issues of social relations, such as race and racism. If it is possible to naturalize a thing, person, group, community and so on, it follows that treating them differently can be achieved easily. The idea here attaches "natural" to the circulation of common sense, which therefore enables communities to become similarly naturalized. Over time this natural quality is maintained on many fronts through repetition. It can be argued that this has been the case with Black community.

Himani Bannerji has used common sense to understand the particular force and pervasiveness of racism. She has argued that common sense is "accretional, and being unthought out it leaves plenty of room for contradiction, myths, guesses and rumours."[12] She goes on to state that it is deeply practical in nature and that "the general direction of its movement as such comes from common socio-economic and cultural practices which, in turn, common sense helps to organize." [13] For Bannerji, epistemological strategies are securely fastened in the common sense of racism. What I would like to take from Bannerji is this idea of the rootedness of knowledge and to what this rooted knowledge is attached, that is, sexism, racism, homophobia and so on. It seems to me that the expression of such rooted knowledge takes shape through these forms of social relations.

What is offered to us, though, is that common sense is a storehouse of knowledges, and, for our purposes, it's what's being stored as knowledge that is important and not so much that common sense is a storehouse. Thinking through the nature of that knowledge and how it has stabilized itself through time and space is important at this conceptual conjuncture, especially since what Black community means is quite mythic — it is a "fiction," as Isaac Julien argues.[14] Lawrence argues that "while common sense embodies the practical experience and solution to the everyday problems encountered by the 'popular masses' throughout their history, it is also shot through with elements and beliefs derived from earlier or other more developed ideologies which have *sedimented* into it."[15] This sedimentation, the staying ability of the commonsensical, can be linked to the formation of the essential. If we are to agree that common sense is not a "unified body of knowledge," then I want to suggest that common sense is a shared mimetic possibility. While common sense is shifting and changing (the un-unified), there is some sense of the common senscial as "same," that "sameness" is the "hearts-of-hearts" knowing, transmittable through time, space, and struggle. It is the common sense sedimentation that shapes the "storehouse," and, by extension, defines what knowledges will narrate or suit each situation. And yet, even as I explore the doubleness of common sense, the very idea of a "storehouse" doesn't get translated in the movement of the idea through space and time. What stays with us are the norms, forms and "hearts-of-hearts" knowledge that make up common sense.

In *Essentially Speaking*, Diana Fuss thinks through the definition of essentialism to argue that "essentialism is classically defined as a belief in true essence — that which is most irreducible, unchanging, and therefore constitutive of a person or thing."[16] Essentialism generally denotes the fixing property of a sign or some unitary characteristic of an object or subject of inquiry. Fuss introduces Locke's arguments on "real" and "nominal" essence in order to develop a tension between constructionists and essentialists. Real essence, coming from Aristotle, signifies the unchanging, whereas nominal essence is a "classificatory fiction,"[17] something which needs a category, label or name. Real essences are products of observation, while nominal essence is derived, or rather assigned, through a system of language. Real essence, Fuss argues, is in fact a nominal essence; that is to say, nominal essence is a "linguist kind, a product of naming" and that despite the slight of differences in their definitions, they both belong to the common classification: essence, they are part of the same "semantic family."[18] Setting up this tightrope act between essentialism and constructionism is in no way suggestive of any easy binary. In fact, we must recognize from a constructionist perspective, that even essences are, in part, constructed. Fuss suggests that maybe it is time "to ask whether essences can change and whether constructions can be normative."[19] This argument falls short of suggesting that it is the sustainability or staying power of essence that makes essentialism so much more concrete. The analysis also leaves out the types of investments made in other societies to ensure the sustained strength of essence.

However, it is the unchanging, unshifting aspect of essence that I would like to link up to the idea of common sense. I think that essence works through a certain appeal, a familiarity — or knowledge, even assumptions of knowledge — of a person or thing, and that in many instances this shared understanding acts to foreclose. So the work of essence is wrapped in a particular legitimation through space and time, somewhat like common sense. When essentialism is at work, catagories of subjects, like the citizen, the immigrant and so on, are rigidly constructed. Taking up the idea of a "foreclosure" in the definition of common sense, community may also be constructed in a similarly rigid and legitimized fashion. What is imperative at this moment is to develop a continuous critical identificatory process, *a politics*, one which is not only counterhegemonic but imaginary.

Gayatri C. Spivak's "strategic essentialism" has complicated the grounds of the project of essence. For Spivak, "strategic essentialism" is a political interjection in the constant play of positionings in representational political activity. She argues that making claims against or for essence is quite contingent and therefore has no guarantees. Yet as a political tactic, the risk of essence may be an important gamble. Effective use of strategy must begin from a located or situated place since "a strategy suits a situation, a strategy is not a theory."[20] The operation of this idea concerns asserting positionality while refusing to simultaneously essentialize it.[21]

Diana Fuss has argued that when practiced by subaltern subjects, the use of this strategy can be exceptionally disruptive, since it "represents an approach which evaluates the motivations behind the deployment of essentialism."[22] However, she reminds us of the dangers of movement from the provisional to the permanent in the use of this interventionary strategy: "there is always a danger that the long-term effect of such a 'temporary' intervention may, in fact, lead once again to a re-entrenchment of a more reactionary form of essentialism."[23] Subject positions remain the telling cost or success of this interventionary strategy: it is about who uses it. For Fuss, the important point remains that the risk of essentialism is worth taking. When Fuss speaks about "risk," I take it to mean a practical ethicality.

If we return to the *Show Boat* experience, what made essence playable was the investment in the struggle against racist oppression; the investment, I believe, was made in the name of local anti-racist practice. This is where my convictions lie when I think about Blackness, community and *Show Boat*. Taking up Blackness, at the time of the mounting of *Show Boat*, as a strategy for addressing the functionality of racism in racist societies, meant that using essence, was a political act, an act of *politics* for movement between essence and strategic essence. This is a methodologic "nomadology" worth sustaining as part of cultural expressivity — in this case Black expressive cultures.

Difference: Thinking Through Black Community

By thinking through the various issues involved in the house of essentialism and common sense, I aim to show that essence cannot construct community and that mimetic desires are unable to hold the line when addressing difference and identity as complex social dynamics. Thinking Black community raises serious issues connected to the debates around both common sense and essence. Black community has become a nebulous entity, one which is identified by the politics of skin more than as a negotiated process. The end result of a sedimentary knowing of Black community is a homogenous, transparent identity category, which offers entrenched and inflexible boundaries. Black community becomes a finished product in that it is thought in advance,[24] and to call on something called the Black community is to perform a set of erasures. Among the disappearing acts within the category Black community is the multiplicity and plurality of ethnic representations,[25] the hybrid and creolized possibilities of identity formations, the embrace of a homoerotic world, the courage to deconstruct masculinity, matriarchy, and so on. The question of difference in this scenario is what I am calling into question. Is difference being thought out in advance — is it preconceived, already organized? For me, what makes an already constituted, commonsensical construct a possibility is only if, for Black community, the stableness of the sign *is* its very meaning. The question then becomes: what are the kinds of commitments brought to bear on Black community that would forget multiple cries for representation. Unity and oneness denies Black community as an open-ended expression.

If we read Black community as a continually shifting possibility, not thought in advance but performed and refashioned as a process of becoming, then the task at hand, in terms of contextualizing Black community, is to read Black community as an imagined and inoperative community. This is why Benedict Anderson's seminal work, *Imagined Communities* is important and vital for thinking through the terrain of Black community. [26] While Anderson's work concentrates on the construction of national identity, it offers us a way of thinking about how community might be imagined. For Anderson, nation is "an imagined political community."[27] In imagining ourselves as community, Anderson argues that it is necessary to envision the possibility of our union: that while "the members of the smallest nation will never know most of their fellow members, meet them, or hear them"... "in the minds of each lies the image of their communion."[28] This understanding of nation posits definable limits that may exhibit elasticity and both certain and uncertain boundaries. Anderson, in his formulation of nation, argues that nation is imagined as a community when a "deep horizontal comradeship," and "fraternity" is conceived. According to Anderson, all communities are imagined, distinguished "not by their falsity/genuineness, but by the style in which they are imagined."[29] This is where Chandra Mohanty's study of Third World women is crucial as a way of opening up categorical certainities.[30] Not only does Mohanty destabilize the very category of "third world women," she borrows Anderson in order to renegotiate categorical practices altogether.

For Mohanty, Anderson's "imagined community" should be refigured as an analytic tool. Mohanty's work charts the complex spaces of identity politics in order to think through an imagined community of Third World oppositional struggles, where the possibility of constructing "potential alliances and collaborations across divisive boundaries" makes thinkable the political commitments of women.[31] Imagined communities, refashioned by Mohanty, shifts attention from "essentialist notions of third world feminist struggles, suggesting political rather than biological or cultural bases for alliance."[32] Along these lines, we can think of imagined communities as politically rather than essentially defined. This framework will enable us to struggle on the very terrain of identity politics, allowing for the complexity that a politics of process can bring.

How Black community is imagined is dependant on the chaotic brilliance of performative acts that take shape at the limits of representation. These performances are in the first instance political acts: political redefinitions of Blackness. While the idea of politics is resonant with Anderson and Mohanty, for Jean-Luc Nancy "the political is the place where community...is brought into play."[33] If we understand the political to be a site of process and deliberate movement, then the question of how community is constituted must be posed in fluid — not essential — terms. Black community must be shifted to emphasize its "communities" aspect. I want to suggest that it is in the spaces of the political that community loses it fixity; where identificatory practices get negotiated in the complex. It is this limit that forges the necessary communicative process that enables community to become.

How community is played out — how it is performed — is an important aspect of its narrative history. Nancy's writing of community has ushered in a welcome disruption of thinking community at its limits. Nancy's rethinking of community as an "unworking," "desoeuvree" questions the desire for mimesis or "immanence." The "unworking" Nancy suggests refers to "that which, before or beyond the work, withdraws from the work, and which, no longer having to do either with production or with completion, encounters interruption, fragmentation, suspension."[34] Working through several complex concepts: singularity, communication, sharing, being-in-common and finitude, Nancy exposes the conventional or normative sense of community as operationalized, as something that "operates." Dennis Foster has argued that the community Nancy imagines, "is one that emerges from what resists the communal, the gathering of all people in an essential spirit." [35] Against the idea of essence, Nancy's "unworking" allows for the possibility of figuring community at its limits.

For Nancy, community is "not a gathering of individuals," rather, it is "to be *in* common, or to be with each other, or to be together."[36] He theorizes togetherness as the outside to an inside, "where without building any common 'inside' it is given as an external interiority."[37] Nancy maintains that this sense of togetherness is not an essence; it is never an essence: it is existence. His conceptualization of togetherness is a mark of otherness. Arguing that togetherness is existence, Nancy adds that, "[t]o exist, therefore, is to hold one's 'selfness' as an 'otherness,'" illustrating that "community is the community of otherness."[38] In this formulation of otherness, there is no commonality. In fact, what Nancy invokes here is his thesis of singularity, of singular beings. Community of otherness is a partaking of otherness. It is the first recognition of difference in his theory of community.

In *The Inoperative Community*, Nancy argues that "community without community is to *come*, in the sense that it is always *coming*, endlessly, at the heart of every collectivity (because it never stops coming), it ceaselessly resists collectivity (homogeneity) itself as much as it resists the individual."[39] What Nancy marks here, besides the calling of community, is that community resists the individual. The individual is "the absolutely detached for-itself, taken as origin and as certainty;"[40] it is atomistic, indivisible. Nancy refers to the individual as the 'figure of immanence.' And while the individual is set in almost opposition to community, Nancy notes, "one cannot make a world with simple atoms."[41] There needs to be a *clinamen*, he argues, an inclination, "from one toward the other, of one by the other, or from one to the other. Community is at least the *clinamen* of the 'individual.'"[42] The individual is read as "being without relation." Since "the individual" connotes a "detached, for itself," and is without relation, "it contradicts itself as a concept: something cannot be separate without being separate from-and therefore in relation to-something else."[43]

While Nancy rejects the concept of "the individual," he replaces it with the idea of singularity. For Nancy singularity has more resonance in the thinking through of community. Singularity is "constitutive of the question of community...it is the reverse of the question of the absolute"[44] — it is *not* being without relation. Nancy designs singular beings or singularity as "finite being," where finite being is not a "detaching," as is "the individual." Singularity is "made up only of the network, the interweaving, and the sharing of singularities."[45] Moving from the atomistic, Nancy contextualizes singularity "as finitude itself: at the end (or at the beginning), with the contact of the skin (or the heart) of another singular being, at the confines of the *same* singularity that is, as such, always *other*, always shared, always exposed."[46] In community, therefore, there can be no singular being without, of course, another singular being. Community is the constitution of singular beings working and sharing together; it is a matter of their communication. In this scheme, Nancy poignantly notes that there is no "communion" of singularities — he means that there is not totality, no immanence (to essence) to which singular beings are bound.

In communication, singular beings expose themselves to each

other: they co-appear (compear). Finitude "exists as communication." But what is finitude? Nancy articulates finitude as "infinitely finite" where we are "infinitely exposed to our existence as a nonessence, infinitely exposed to the otherness of our 'own' being."[47] Finitude is the "togetherness of otherness;" it is, therefore, not an "enclosed form," nor a closure but singular beings in exposition through communication to an "outside." The outside of which Nancy speaks is "another exposition" of another singularity, "the same other." What occurs in this exposition (which seems like a continuous exposing) is "a mutual interpellation of singularities prior to any address in language."[48] Communication is always an exposition. But Nancy is quick to warn us that communication is not a bond. Compearance, to co-appear, is "the *between* as such: you *and* I (between us) — a formula in which the *and* does not imply juxtaposition, but exposition."[49] Nancy maintains that communication is exposition; the definitive constitution of singularity to an outside.

Community, then, is not something to be worked out; it is not a project in that sense. As a result, there can be no fusion of singular beings, no communion, since singularities must co-appear, they must expose one to the other. A communion or totality would resemble an essence of community. Community is a gift, Nancy says, one which is given and one which must be communicated.[50] Nancy leaves us with a challenge by suggesting that, "[w]e have to decide — and decide how to-be in common, to allow our existence to exist. This is not only at each moment a political decision; it is a decision about politics, about if and how we allow our otherness to exist, to inscribe itself as community."[51]

Nancy gives us one possible way to think community outside of mimetic desirings. His formulation helps us to contend with the tension in the movement from *the* (essential) Black community to a *(be)coming* community. *Becoming* community is always already a performative in process. Moreover, Nancy allows us to unthink the spaces of "the common" to question (comm)unity as well as the uncommonality of community. And this is key for thinking Black communities: can an uncommonality also form community? In other words, can what is *unlike* craft a common? A reading of Nancy provokes the question of the place of difference in the project of community.

With this in mind, a careful consideration of the Black community at the height of the *Show Boat* debacle is a question of the inoperative: was inoperative community performed? No; and reading Nancy shows us why. However, to achieve inoperative community, there must be a desire to always expose Blackness, essence, authenticity; it is about chaos and the living of anxieties as much a problematization of Blackness. As long as the story of community remains within borders of familiarity, what will take place is a worked out, and therefore simple, understanding of community.

And so, in terms of community, and *the* Black community in particular, the *Show Boat* production was a missed chance at a strategic reconfiguration of what it means to "be together" in the Nancian sense. The co-appearance that occured during the *Show Boat* demonstrations was based on a preconceived community, a community that could be called up at will. I call this the "dormancy" of community because it refuses alterity as part of the equation of cultural politics. The very conditions upon which singularity is made possible is in fact a demand of difference. *Show Boat* could not accomodate the communicative process necessary for singular beings to work an interiority.

De-essentializing Black Community: Strategic Essentialism, Politics or Pragmatics

> Basically, in the work that I do, I try to produce a critical self-reflexive response. I think Blackness is a term used — in the way that terms like "the Black community" or "Black folk" are usually bandied about — to exclude others who are part of that community.[52]

Isaac Julien's comments immediately frame a postmodern possibility for approaching the integral, interconnected and intricate tendrils of identity and difference. The question for Black community is whether a multiplicitous identificatory structure of thinking itself can be avowed. The genealogy charted in this paper brings us to this very question. Reading Nancy provides us with an approach; one way in which the myriad voices on the margins of Black community can be represented democratically to allow for an imagined visioning of community to take place. In fact, Nancy offers a politics of community that would be able to deconstruct what is being disavowed at the core construction of the Black community. This is why thinking a strategic essentialism might be a methodological possibility if community is continuously being made. Strategic essentialism allows us to accentuate the importance of signifying practices without getting fixed on a particular sign; meaning making is made contingent. So, what is at stake here is whether a politics that invites a strategic essentialism to the table is able to move beyond the essence of strategic essentialism to the laudability of the strategy. I believe that strategic essentialism is a pragmatic and cautious approach through which various communities are able to enhance quality of life.

Nancy's project situates the question of difference within the politics of communities. This politics suggests that we must always be able to understand the provisional grounds around identity, as well as the sheer complexity of identity classifications. I would very much like to read Nancy within the scheme outlined by Cornel West in his seminal piece "The New Cultural Politics of Difference."[53] For West, the new cultural politics of difference includes three features:

> to thrash the monolithic and homogenous in the name of diversity, multiplicity and heterogeneity; to reject the abstract, general and universal in light of the concrete, specific and particular; and to historicize, contextualize and pluralize by highlighting the contingent, provisional, variable, tentative, shifting and changing.[54]

Working through this framework, activists, cultural workers, artists, academics and so on, can demonstrate a narrative of community that is unfinished, open, and negotiable. This is what Nancy positions as the "unworking." Community is a continuous unworking.

Endnotes

1. See Carol Tator, Frances Henry and Winston Mattis, *Challenging Racism in the Arts: Case Studies of Controversy and Conflict* (Toronto: University of Toronto Press, 1998); M. Nourbese Philip, *Showing Grit* (Toronto: Poui Productions, 1993).

2. See bell hooks, *Killing Rage: Ending Racism* (New York: Henry Holt and Company, 1995). Her chapter "Black Identity: Liberating Subjectivity" is important as it shows how this process happened historically in shaping community and African-American identity.

3. See Stuart Hall, "What is This 'Black' in Black Popular Culture," in Gina Dent, ed., *Black Popular Culture* (Seattle: Bay Press, 1992).

4. Stuart Hall, "What is This 'Black'," 32.

5. See Manthia Diawara, "Black Studies, Cultural Studies, Performative Acts," in Cameron McCarthy and Warren Crichlow, eds., *Race and Representation in Education* (New York: Routledge, 1993).

6. See Errol Lawrence "Just plain common sense: the roots of racism," in the Birmingham Centre for Cultural Studies, ed., *The Empire Strikes Back: Race and Racism in 1970s Britain* (London: Hutchinson, 1983).

7. Errol Lawrence, "Just plain common sense," 48.

8. Errol Lawrence, "Just plain common sense," 49. Note: in this citation Lawrence is himself paraphrasing from two authors: M. Baker and Hall, Lumley and McLennan. For further citation please refer to Lawrence's work.

9. Chris Weedon, *Feminist Practice & Poststructuralist Theory*, 77.

10. Ibid.

11. Ibid

12. See Himani Bannerji, "Introducing Racism: Notes Towards an Anti-Racist Feminism," in *Resources for Feminist Research* 16, no. 1 (March, 1987): 10.

13. Himani Bannerji, "Introducing Racism," 10.

14. See "Discussion," in Gina Dent, ed., *Black Popular Culture* (Seattle: Bay Press, 1992).

15. Himani Bannerji, "Introducing Racism," 49.

16. Diana Fuss, *Essentially Speaking: Feminism, Nature and Difference* (New York: Routledge, 1989), 2.

17. Diana Fuss, *Essentially Speaking*, 4.

18. Diana Fuss, *Essentially Speaking*, 5.

19. Diana Fuss, *Essentially Speaking*, 6.

20. See Ellen Rooney with Gayatri C. Spivak, "In a Word: Interview," in Naomi Schor and Elizabeth Weed, *The Essential Difference* (Bloomington: Indiana Press, 1994), 157.

21. See Ellen Rooney in her interview with Spivak (see footnote 21),157.

22. Diana Fuss, "Reading Like a Feminist," in Naomi Schor and Elizabeth Weed, *The Essential Difference*,(Bloomington: Indiana Press, 1994), 107.

23. Diana Fuss, "Reading," 107-108.

24. See Judith Butler, "Contingent Foundations: Feminism and the Question of 'Postmodernism,'" in Judith Butler and Joan W. Scott, eds., *Feminists Theorize the Political* (New York: Routledge, 1992).

25. Specific to ethnicity, Black community has always been read in binary terms. While I speak about the various erasures which occur at/in the moment of essence, I need to be clear about the social relations of racism and power at play in the context of racist national imaginaries not unlike that of Canada. Set against whiteness and in relation to legacies (past and present) of colonialism and imperial strategies which continue to linger about us, Blackness is robbed of its plurality and heterogeneity.

26. See Benedict Anderson, *Imagined Communities: Reflections on the Origin and Spread of Nationalism* (London: Verso, 1983).

27. Benedict Anderson, *Imagined Communities*, 7.

28. Benedict Anderson, *Imagined Communities*, 6.

29. Benedict Anderson, *Imagined Communities*, 6.

30. See in particular, Chandra T. Mohanty, "Cartographies of Struggle: Third World Women and the Politics of Feminism," in Chandra Talpade Mohanty, Ann Russo, Lordes Torres, eds., *Third World Women and the Politics of Feminism* (Bloomington: Indiana University Press, 1991).

31. Chandra Mohanty, "Cartographies of Struggle," 4.

32. Chandra Mohanty, "Cartographies of Struggle," 4.

33. See Jean-Luc Nancy, *The Inoperative Community*, ed., Peter Connor, trans.m Peter Connor, Lisa Garbos, Michael Holland and Simona Sawhney (Minneapolis: University of Minnesota Press, 1991), xxxvii.

34. Jean-Luc Nancy, *The Inoperative Community*, 31.

35. See Dennis A. Foster, "Pleasure and Community in Cultural Criticism," in *American Literary History*, vol. 6, no. 2 (Summer), 375.

36. See Jean-Luc Nancy, "Finite History," in David Carroll ed., *The States of "Theory": History, Art, and Critical Discourse* (New York: Columbia University Press, 199), 159.

37. Jean-Luc Nancy, "Finite History," 160.

38. Jean-Luc Nancy, "Finite History," 160.

39. Jean-Luc Nancy, *The Inoperative Community*, 71.

40. See Jean-Luc Nancy, *The Inoperative Community*, 3. See also Gillian Rose, "Performing Inoperative Community: the space and the resistance of some community arts projects," in Steve Pile and Michael Keith, eds., *Geographies of Resistance*, (New York: Routledge, 1997),184-202.

41. Jean-Luc Nancy, *The Inoperative Community*, 3.

42. Jean-Luc Nancy, *The Inoperative Community*, 3-4.

43. See Kathleen Dow, "Ex-Posing Identity: Derrida and Nancy on the (im)Possibility," in *Philosophy and Social Criticism*,19, no. 3&4. p.263. I am indebted to Dow's work in this essay. She explains Nancy with utter easy and with brilliant clarity, making some of the most unreadable philosophy quite accessible.

44. Jean-Luc Nancy, *The Inoperative Community*, 6.

45. Jean-Luc Nancy, *The Inoperative Community*, 27.

46. Jean-Luc Nancy, *The Inoperative Community*, 28.

47. Jean-Luc Nancy, "Finite History," 161.

48. Jean-Luc Nancy, *The Inoperative Community*, 28.

49. Jean-Luc Nancy, *The Inoperative Community*, 29.

50. Jean-Luc Nancy, *The Inoperative Community*, 35

51. Jean-Luc Nancy, "Finite History," 171.

52. Isaac Julien's response in "Discussion," in Gina Dent, ed., *Black Popular Culture*, 247.

53. Cornell West, "The New Cultural Politics of Difference," in John Rajchman, ed., *The Identity in Question* (New York: Routledge, 1995).

54. Cornel West, "The New Cultural Politics of Difference," 146.

Reckless Eyeballing:
Being Reena in Canada

Tess Chakkalakal

On November 14, 1997 Reena Virk was surrounded and beaten by eight teens underneath a bridge in suburban Victoria, B.C. She survives swarming but is assaulted a second time by others and is found dead in the Victoria Gorge waterway a week later.

Instead of obliterating the possibility of responses paralyzing the addressee with fear, the threat may well be countered by a difficult kind of performative act, one that exploits the redoubled action of the threat (what is intentionally and non-intentionally performed in any speaking), to turn one part of that speaking against the other, confounding the performative power of the threat. — Judith Butler, *Excitable Speech,*1997.

According to Reena Virk's parents, Suman and Manjit, "Reena had low self-esteem and was very insecure." Guy Lawson reports in *Gentleman's Quarterly* (February, 1999) that Reena had been teased by the other girls since she started school. "Reena was ugly. She had hair on her face. She was East Indian." Further accounts of the Reena Virk case corroborate Lawson's reportage. In a CBC documentary, Leslie MacKinnon explains that at school Virk was constantly being teased and bullied. They made fun of the way she looked — her weight, her dark complexion. In a feature article for *Saturday Night Magazine* ("Who Was Reena Virk?" April, 1998) Sid Tafler explains that Virk was targeted by bullies and constantly humiliated by her peers. Virk's unusual bodily features became the source of a number of what Tafler refers to as, "nicknames": "Daddy," "the ugly," "bearded lady," and "beast."

Six teenagers have been convicted of assault causing bodily harm and two others have been convicted of second-degree murder. All those involved in the killing of Reena Virk were under the age of eighteen, therefore little is known of their identities. This chapter reflects on the Reena Virk case by asking a simple, if unanswerable, question: at what point does name-calling, teasing and bullying become insufficient? At what point, in other words, is it necessary for verbal abuse to become physical death?

When the story of Reena Virk's death first became available for public consumption, the Canadian news media was concerned with more pressing questions: "why is violence among girls sharply on the rise? And what, if anything, can be done to halt the trend?" (Patricia Chisholm, "Bad Girls" *Maclean's*, December 1997). By way of investigative reporting and analysis, the media found answers. Expert witnesses, namely Sybille Artz, Director of the School of Child and Youth Care at the University of Victoria and author of *Sex, Power & the Violent School Girl* (1997), produced documented evidence that Virk's death was caused by the increasing pressures on young girls to be more powerful. Furthermore, Virk's murder, brutal and disturbing as it was for *all* Canadians, was part of a "trend" of rising instances of violence among "girls." In conjunction with their reports on the Reena Virk case, the Canadian news media provided readers with a series of statistics. *The Alberta Report*'s coverage of the trial of the girls, who pleaded not guilty to the charges of assault causing bodily harm, provide a series of statistics to help readers contextualize the case. "In 1996," they told us, "the number of Canadian teens charged with violent offences had more than tripled from a decade earlier. By this century it is expected that the population of the high-crime bracket of fourteen to twenty-four-year-olds will have climbed by more than eight hundred thousand to 5.2 million.

You do the math: in a population of roughly twenty-five million with 5.2 million incidents of violent offences, the odds of being involved in a violent crime are pretty high. Something, clearly, needs to be done to curb this "trend." Yet, when experts like Sybille Artz of the University of Victoria and Rosemary Gartner, professor of sociology at the University of Toronto and author of *The Crime Conundrum* are asked, they say that there are "no historical examples to match the viciousness of the Virk beating, nor any past examples of teenagers swarming their victims that has precipitated such a response from the Canadian public." When asked about the disjunction between the statistics and the "facts" of the Reena Virk case, Professor Gartner is quoted as saying, "I don't know why people perceive an increase in crime. I don't believe the Canadian public is totally irrational. It's an interesting question," (see Alberta Report, v. 25, February 23, 1998). It is indeed an interesting question. The question is: why Reena Virk? What was so different about Reena Virk that precipitated such "viciousness"? Rather than providing a mere example of teen or girl violence, my discussion of the Reena Virk case confronts the problem of the increased "viciousness" that sets this case apart from other instances of "teen violence." In order to consider the particularity of this case, I draw upon Judith Butler's "politics of the performative": a theory of the cause and effect of injurious language in everyday life. While Butler's theory is crucial in formulating an answer to Gartner's "interesting question," the case also reveals certain blindnesses in Butler's theory. I point out these blindnesses in her theory not as a means of discounting it from critical practice but, rather, in order to widen the scope of Butler's theory of performative politics to enable its transformative possibilities.

In *Excitable Speech: A Politics of the Performative* (1997), Judith Butler draws upon J.L. Austin's theory of illocutionary and perlocutionary speech acts to show the "multiple possibilities" available to individuals subjected to verbal abuse or injurious language. Butler's politics of the performative insists on the possibility of agency for the subjugated. A refusal on the part of the subject to allow injurious language to have its desired effect enables the subject to move beyond certain institutional and systemic constraints.

If we apply Butler's theory of performative language to the Reena Virk case, we are forced to confront the names she was called prior to her death. What was the force of these names in constituting this particular subject? According to Butler, these names had little to do with Virk's constitution. Whether or not Virk was insecure as a result of being called these names is difficult to determine. Nonetheless, we can speculate that, based on available testiminies, these names did not procure their intended effect. That is, Reena Virk appears not to have listened to these names — she acted as if she was not an "ugly," "East Indian," "a bearded lady," "a freak." She acted as if she had power, as if she could do things that a girl of her size, colour and ethnicity was clearly prohibited from doing.

The increased viciousness of the Reena Virk case provoked a series articles, television reports and documentaries on the case. Due to the stipulations of the Young Offenders Act, the names and identities of those tried and prosecuted in the Reena Virk case remain unknown.

The details of Virk's life and death provide an ample substitute for this lack of information. Reena's parents, Suman and Manjit Virk — we learned — "have a more rigid belief system than many people. Not only were they members of Victoria's East Indian community, they were also practicing Jehovah's Witnesses. Her parents were thus 'overprotective.'" "For Reena," Sandra Martin reports in *Chatelaine*'s May 1998 issue, "life at home was stifling. She wanted to stay out past her 9 p.m. curfew and to hang around in the park with kids who smoked cigarettes and marijuana and who didn't feel the tug of such a parental lash," (*Chatelaine*, v. 71(5) My '98 pg 70-77). Who might these kids "who didn't feel the tug of such a parental lash" be? Kids who were different from Reena: white kids. When grounded, Reena ran away from home; when her parents imposed further restrictions, Reena did the unthinkable: she broke with her family altogether and, hence, with her East Indian/Jehovah's Witness heritage. By accusing her own father of abuse, Reena found the freedom she was so desperately seeking: she was taken from her home and put in foster care. In Martin's words, " Reena had gone from a strictly supervised situation to largely setting her own limits — like a kid with a learner's permit who suddenly finds herself behind the wheel of a high-powered car roaring down the highway at 200 kilometres an hour."

The girls charged with assault and murder in the Reena Virk case explain the motive behind the killing. Reena performed oral sex on one of the girls' boyfriends — and bragged about it. Reena stole an address book of another girl to get phone numbers. She started making calls, calling up boys and asking them out. This isn't the behaviour of an insecure girl, but it is decidedly improper behaviour: improper for a fat, ugly, dark complexioned girl to think that she could *act* like other girls. The Reena Virk case thus provides us with an instance of injurious language in which the subject instigates the failure of the call — in which the subject acts with agency.

What makes the Reena Virk case exemplary, then, is the fact that it provides an instance of Butler's theory of agency — the radical possibilities of the failed performative. But it also points out a failure in Butler's theory of agency. That is, Butler's theory presents a kind of "romantic" or "utopian" vision that renders the multiple possibilities of her "Politics of the Performative," sadly, ineffectual. While she concedes that in being called an injurious name, one is derogated and demeaned, these negative results are, in her formation, overshadowed by the triumph of the agential subject. For Butler, injurious names hold out an added dimension of possibility for the subject: by being called an injurious name one is also paradoxically given a certain possibility for social existence, an initiation into a temporal life of language that exceeds the prior purposes that animate that originary call. So far so good. The problem is, what happens to the name-caller(s) while the subject of the call is experiencing the multiple possibilities of the injurious address? Butler neglects the status of the oppressor — for good reason. Oppressors have been occupying a position in the limelight for far too long. But such a neglect has serious repercussions for Butler's newly constituted agential subject. If the subordinate subject refuses the call and creates a set of conditions that oppose her callers address, her callers may respond in kind. A struggle for power ensues in which the original name-callers find creative ways to break down the subject's resistance. Creative, in the Reena Virk case, is simply another term for the "viciousness" of this particular "total speech situation" (Austin's term).

Butler is thus unable to cope with this new total speech situation: one that must now deal with the terms of agency and its rather undesirable effects. What happens after the subject refuses to respond to her name-callers? The Reena Virk case offers a grim, but all too real response: death. While I feel that Butler's politics of the performative falls short of addressing the conditions of the Reena Virk case, I do believe that her theory opens up the possiblity for a critical response to this case, and a response to the media's reactionary deployment of it.

I am suggesting that the only possiblity for an affirmative mode of response — in the case of injurious language or what is more commonly referred to as verbal abuse — is not a reversal or failure of the speech act; but, instead, a *redeployment* of language that comes to terms with the names involved in the Reena Virk case which, in effect, make the case more spectacular. By using language in such a way as to make it impossible for the case *not* to be forgotten. Using language, in other words, to record the case as a historical precedent. I want to open the possibility for agency in the Reena Virk case by calling it by its proper name: a Canadian lynching.

In order to do so, I first want to cite two contemporary redeployments of the term lynching: Ishmael Reed's 1986 novel, *Reckless Eyeballing*, and the Clarence Thomas Hearings, which took place in 1992. On one hand, the Thomas/Hill proceedings were yet another instance in the US's illustrious history of sexual harassment defaming the virtue of a male public figure. Yet Clarence Thomas used the term lynching in his defense case: to allow Anita Hill's testimony to be heard, Thomas argued, was to sacrifice him for a crime he did not commit. To allow Anita Hill's testimony to be heard, Thomas insisted, was to mock the protocols of judicial procedure. To allow Anita Hill's testimony to be heard, Thomas accused, was to "destroy" him. To "caricature" him. To "lynch" him. And history would not repeat itself in his instance: Thomas would refuse — as thousands of men before him had, in vain, tried to do — to yield the truth in terms of his body.

Ishmael Reed provides a similar deployment of the term. He uses the term in his novel to undercut the power, to borrow his terminology, of "angry feminists." According to Reed's novel, the concept of reckless eyeballing most significantly refers to the charge historically made against African American men who are caught (or imagined to be) staring at white women. Of course, in Reed's novel, as in real life the significance of this accusation is that it provides a reasonable motive for lynching. In Reed's novel this accusation is made within the protagonist, Ian Ball's play about Ham Hill. In this play, which Ball wrote to appease feminists who "sex-listed" him as a result of his misogynistic first play, Ham Hill is a young African American who is lynched for "eyeballing" a white woman. Ball's play is loosely based on the 1955 lynching of Emmett Till of Chicago. In 1955, fourteen-year-old Till, who was visiting relatives in Mississippi, was lynched for allegedly whistling at a white woman, Carolyn Bryant. The lynchers, Bryant's husband and his half-brother, were acquitted. While loosely based on this event, Ball's play, as the play's director in the novel explains, offers a twist: "He has the woman the kid allegedly stared at demand that his body be exhumed so that the corpse can be tried. She wants to erase any doubt in the public's mind that she was not the cause of the eyeballing she got" (39-41). Reed's deployment of the term in his novel, like Thomas's invocation of the term during the hearings, illuminates that as much as lynching is a term of racial significance it also carries a great deal of weight in the war between the sexes.

If lynching is done to the male body, is it possible for a female body to be lynched? Both Clarence Thomas and Ishmael Reed's radical redeployment of the term, prove that women — white or — are as capable of lynching as white men. Given the intersection of race, or more accurately, ethnicity, gender, and sexuality in the Reena Virk case, the term lynching — in its contemporary *decontextualized* manifestations, makes sense. The question now becomes, to what effect?

Regardless of their political biases, both Thomas's and Reed's deployment of the term broadens our understanding of the relationship between racial violence and the representations of it. In a Canadian lynching, such as the Reena Virk Case, the terms and forms of violence metamorphose. Explicit mention of racism as a contributing factor in any case is often met with a healthy dose of skepticism. Acts of racial violence, in Canada, tend to disappear from the public mind. The first and only public mention of "race" in the Reena Virk case appeared in the February 1999 issue of GQ — an American publication — by Guy Lawson. According to Lawson, "most of the girls who attacked Reena were white, but it was an article of faith for officials that it had nothing to do with race" (165, February 1999).

Despite their desire to suppress any mention of "race," the Canadian news media unwittingly use Reena Virk's ethnic identity as a source of her own insecurity that becomes a factor or "motive" in her death. As the Reena Virk case became a "media story" the logic of Canadian racism was slowly revealed: it is so deeply ingrained in our national psyche that locating its operative features in certain situations is deemed superfluous. Racism is a feature of everyday Canadian life.

Calling this event a lynching opens up the possibility of interpreting and locating the effects of Canadian racism. Considering it both an aberration in and the culmination of the logic of racism, lynching is also commonly interpreted as a false act; that is to say, the deaths it causes are presumed to be unjust because history has shown us that the alleged violations typically never occurred or were wrongly defined in the first place. It is crucial to call the Reena Virk case by its proper name, so that it may affect our view of the way racism works in Canada. It is clear that the case has been erroneously construed by the Canadian news media as a sensational example of the rising trend in "teen" violence, an error that has systematically erased Reena Virk's death at the hand of racists from everday life in Canada.

Works Cited

Butler, Judith P. *Excitable Speech: a politics of the performative.* Routledge: New York, 1997.

Reed, Ishamael. *Reckelss Eyeballing.* St. Martin's Press: New York, 1986.

Impossible to Occupy:
André Alexis's *Childhood*

Leslie Sanders

Normative subject-positions are rendered impossible for the black subject-position to occupy. — Kobena Mercer

On a certain level, *Childhood* is all about Trinidad. But it's never stated. It's one of the hidden things...there but not here. — André Alexis

The most celebrated work of fiction yet by an African Canadian is André Alexis's first novel, *Childhood*, published in 1998. Nominated for the Giller Prize, tied with Alice Munro's *The Love of a Good Woman* for the Trillium, and winner of the Chapters/Books in Canada First Novel Award, *Childhood* has already appeared in more than six foreign editions. Alexis was not unknown before the publication of *Childhood*. He had already published a collection of short stories called *Despair and other stories of Ottawa* (1994), and had two of his plays performed. And upon his move to Toronto from Ottawa, he had taken up the role of gadfly/provocateur, challenging Canadian Black writers to look to their own communities for inspiration, rather than south of the border. In his review of Dionne Brand's essay collection *Bread out of Stone* for the *Globe and Mail* for example, Alexis admonished his two-time countrywoman (Trinidad and Canada) to be less angry and critical, and more appreciative of Canada. In this review and elsewhere, Alexis seems uncomfortable with the open critique of Canadian racism that marks so many representations of Canada in work by his Black contemporaries, not only those born in the Caribbean. Yet Alexis has, on occasion, turned his attention to the general issue of African Canadian writing.

In "Borrowed Blackness" Alexis examines his own sense of difference from US culture, generally, and from its racial discourse in particular. He writes:

> [T]here's an absence I feel at the heart of much Black Canadian art. I miss hearing Black Canadians speak *from* Canada. I miss hearing Black Canadian writing that is conscious of Canada, writing that speaks not just about situation, or about the earth, but rather *from* the earth. After all, it is our country, and it is our responsibility to add our voices to the white voices that are articulating Canada...less to the land as physical reality than imagined possibility, and to speak of the imagination's place in the creation of a shared world...[t]o be a Black artist is to have, almost inevitably, to deal with being "Black," to deal with social reality, though that too is a possibility of place, I think (Alexis, 1995: 20).

Alexis's insistence on possibility, and on the importance of "adding in our voices to the white voices that are articulating Canada" bespeaks confidence about his place in the nation. Trinidadian-born, Alexis came to Canada when he was four. Unlike most prominent, Caribbean-born Black Canadian writers then, Alexis grew to maturity in Canada the only place — at least publically — with which he identifies himself. His quarrel with Brand had disturbing undertones of the paternalist nation that expects gratitude from its immigrants. However, it may not signal that so much as a desire to be a writer whose race "adds another dimension" to the possibilities of reading his work rather, than having his race overdetermine how it is read, or the politics of his expression. His resistance, then, is to being categorized along with writers who have no such fears. [1] In "Crossroads: seeing art as politics ought to make it controversial: then why is it so easy to ignore?", Alexis concludes by saying: "[The work of video artist Stan Douglas] represents, as does the poetry of George Elliott Clarke and Clement Virgo's eye, the beginnings of an aesthetic force that needs no defence. *It has to be met on the ground it sets for us, not the ground we set for it* [emphasis added]." The group of Black artists Alexis names are heterogeneous in terms of their history of attachment to Canada. The "we" with which the article concludes is therefore strangely ambiguous. In a recent interview, Alexis argues that he has sought no profile as a "Black writer," and feels no obligation to discuss race if he chooses not to (Redhill).

Given Alexis's belief that the project of Black Canadian artists speaks from a distinctive ground, it is notable that reviewers have, by and large, read race in *Childhood* as incidental, rather than intrinsic. This is perhaps not surprising, since unlike most of his contemporaries, Alexis underplays racial issues; or, more accurately, he rarely draws attention to the Blackness of his Black characters.[2] Typically – but not always — their Blackness is naturalized: a footnote — at times a literal footnote — to the narrative. This silence concerning race may parallel the polite and understated ways in which Canadian racism is often expressed. It may comprise an experiment, an investigation into whether "race matters" when a Black voice articulates the nation.[3] It may also suggest a profound sense of ambivalence about the place and space of "race" in the present-day nation. In relation to this issue, Alexis reminds interviewer Michael Redhill that the narrator of *Childhood* is writing his recollections for someone who knows he is Black, and so, mentioning it is unnecessary. Yet the narrator's silence also suggests an unwillingness to see his race is a factor in the painful confusion that filled his childhood. My analysis of *Childhood* will focus on the novel's (in)attention to race, reading the passivity and spiritual emptiness of its pedantic and repressed central character as connected to his uncertain relationship to his racial origins, and to the ambiguity of the meaning of his Black body in the nation in which he imagines himself.

Typically, in African diasporic autobiography or autobiographical fiction, understanding race and racism is intrinsic to the exercise of self-creation. Alexis himself has commented that Black writers are not formative for him because he did not encounter them in his years of prodigious reading (Gorjup Branko). Yet *Childhood* seems almost deliberately to go up against that tradition. In *Childhood*, race is elusive — in a novel full of interrogation, it is not explicitly examined. Nevertheless, it is clear that in *Childhood* issues of race and abandonment are connected, and that abandonment fills the novel and provides its emotional resonance. Like race, it is everywhere, and like race, it too is not directly interrogated. These two issues, then, comprise what is "not said;" together, I will argue, they provide ways to read the racial in *Childhood*.

Speaking with the Black journalist Donna Nurse, Alexis reveals aspects of his past that he had not to other interviewers. He recalls his fear and confusion when, several years after their immigration to Canada, his parents sent for him, age four, and his sister, who had been left with their grandmother. Now a parent himself, Alexis claims the fatherhood perspective has helped him realize "that when my parents left me behind in Trinidad there was good reason for it. And not only was there good reason for it, it was one of the best things my parents did for me. They did absolutely right." Yet the complexity of the common experience of children whose parents immigrate from the Caribbean and then send for them resonates in *Childhood*.[4]

Alexis's writerly voice is distinctive. His elegant, simple and yet profoundly unsettling style is decidedly modernist and self-consciously deliberate. In his short story collection, *Despair and Other Stories of Ottawa*, the characters have unaccountable experiences, and die strangely. Distress of soul is palpable, if never exactly characterized, and seems to find resonance in vaguely untoward happenings. The Soucoyant[5] in the opening story of *Despair*, who devours her live-in handyman, is a concrete peril; she is comforting and accountable, compared to the threats in the stories that follow. Alexis's tone in the short stories might be described as Franz Kafka and Julio Cortazar by way of the X-files: dispassionately self-involved, and obsessed with both explication and its impossibility.

Where the short stories fixate on the unaccountable, *Childhood* is shows a preoccupation with the desire to account for a life. The novel's conceit, as well as its genre, is fictional autobiography. Its central character, Thomas McMillan, purports to be writing to his lover Marya. He is seeking to understand "Love" by investigating the one relationship in which he thinks he has observed it; that is, in the relationship between his mother Katarina and her friend Henry Wing. The details of McMillan's "singular" childhood, as he calls it, are painful. Born in Petrolia, Ontario, Thomas is abandoned by his mother at birth, and raised by his Trinidadian-born grandmother, a retired schoolteacher, a formidable personality but, in her later years, slovenly alcoholic. When he is ten, his grandmother dies. His mother reappears, ostensibly taking him off to Montreal to begin a new life with her partner of the moment, Mr. Mataf. However, their relationship dissolves halfway across the province. So, Thomas and

Katarina end up in Ottawa, guests of Henry Wing, a mixed race (Black and Chinese) Trinidadian gentleman, who is devoted to Katarina, despite her ambivalence toward him. Thomas's autobiographical attempt to comprehend and order his existence takes place six months after the death both of his mother and, a day later, of Henry Wing. Thomas has inherited Wing's home, and the remnants of Wing's life have become his context.

The novel opens with: "It has been six months since my mother died; a shade less since Henry passed. In that time, I've stayed home and I've kept things tidy." Thomas presents himself as desperately in need of ordering. His principal device is to schedule his apparently uneventful life. These schedules recur throughout the novel. The first schedule he reports is by the hour:

> You have to break the day into manageable portions, and that takes a clock and a little resolve.
> It takes a timetable:
> 7 O'Clock: I am awakened by the alarm.
> 8 O'Clock: I clean my bedroom.
> 9 O'Clock: I feed Alexander (seed)...
> 5 O'Clock (PM): I read the newspaper.
> 6 O'Clock (PM): I read philosophy.
> 7 O'Clock (PM): I continue to read...(3-4).

It is an improvement, we are told, over an earlier version, which attempted to chart his day by the minute. Recognizing the limitations of scheduling, he concludes, "Writing is the discipline I need." The divisions of his narrative are also "disciplinary": "History," "Geography," "the Sciences," and "Housecleaning," he names them, the last a somewhat chilling title, for in it Thomas covers the years after he begins living on his own. Its principal events are the deaths of Katarina and Henry.[6]

Ordering and interpretive strategies pervade his narrative: graphs, charts, theorems, lists and textual exegeses; outlines with subheadings, dictionary definitions, footnotes, mappings. All are brought to bear on the events of Thomas MacMillan's life.[7] These heuristics are often witty, but their speculations produce no insights. Rather, they accentuate Thomas's incomprehension, his over-intellectualizing, and his lack of self-knowledge. Commensurately, this compulsive detailing highlights his estrangement, because he brings it to bear on everything but those things that cause him pain: his loneliness and neglect. He is never angry, although he has ample reason to be mirroring the profoundly unreasoning way of the infant denied the breast.

Virtually nothing in Thomas's childhood was nurturing.

When [my grandmother] was really depressed, there was no telling what breakfast would be like. I had Pablum for breakfast until I was seven years old, so the Pablum was a sure thing. Sometimes she fed me herself. Sometimes she put a bowl of Pablum before me. Sometimes she gave me a spoon, sometimes a fork. And once, in a fit of giddiness, she used her wood spoon as a catapult and fired the warm Pablum at me from the pot. Much of how the day turned out was determined by breakfast"(6).

In his disturbingly objective way, Thomas understands that he was a burden to his grandmother, not the project she wished to take up in her retirement. Thomas's grandmother, Mrs. Edna MacMillan, came from Trinidad, a fact that the narrative first lets slip in a footnote which is also the first inkling given the reader of Thomas's racial origins. In the footnote, he relates the punishing way in which his grandmother taught him to read, adding that she also taught him French, hence he "speak[s] with a Trinidad accent" (15). So minor is the comment that it is easily missed. Moreover, although she dominates the first decade of Thomas's life, he gives Edna only one linguistically indeterminate speaking line — "Clever monkey" — her response when, to avoid having a frying pan thrown at him, Thomas recites a verse of poetry by her favorite poet, Archibald Lampman. At one point, Thoms reflects: "Petrolia crushed everything else from her so thoroughly that I could not guess her origins were anything but Canadian" (29). If Edna sounded Trinidadian, we do not hear it.

Predictably, "race" exists outside the house, but it is unremarkable – perhaps even taboo — within it. If his Blackness has no meaning for Thomas, it does for white Petrolia. A child who frequently visits his neighbours, the Goodmans, calls him "nigger." Yet, according to Thomas, Mr. Goodman dislikes him for reasons he attributes to everything but racism. Speaking of what he gleaned about his mother from another neighbour, Lillian (Martin) Schwartz, Thomas records: "Mrs. Martin was wary of a certain tendency in Negroes, a tendency that was sure to show itself, however good Katarina might appear on the surface. Katarina was even darker than Edna, and look at Edna...she had hoodwinked people into treating her white, and no good came of that"(39). Elsewhere, the same woman expresses concern that her daughter's friend would soon start "acting Black." The most chilling evidence of racism occurs when Thomas wakes one morning to find his grandmother dead. He rushes next door, but when Mr. Goodman opens the door and hears the news, he only promises to come over, and shuts the door, leaving ten-year-old Thomas to return home alone and wander the house for what seems to him like hours.

At one point in this section, Thomas reflects:

My grandmother was a frightening woman, but even she occasionally lost herself in good humour...Petrolia was unexciting, but it was also a stillness: an impossibly delicate tree frog in the palm of my hand, milkweeds, and thistles, acres and acres of green and ochre, the dark stubble that sticks out from under snow-flattened fields...I might even has said my early childhood was good, if I hadn't decided to write it, to write about the others who populated it (23).[8]

Yet he concludes his "History" with a list of his losses when his mother takes him anyway. The final statement: "A community to which, despite myself, I almost belonged" (75) aptly records the meagerness of his expectations. And of his grandmother he says:

She fed me, provided a home of sorts, did what she could for me in her lucid moments, and did no irreparable harm in her moments of abandon...If she couldn't quite love me, that wasn't entirely her fault. Besides, despite all that passed between us, I loved her. How could it be otherwise? For ten years, what tenderness I knew, infrequent though it was, came from her. When she died, I was heartbroken (63).

If "History" located Thomas, however tenuously, in a community, *Childhood*'s second section, "Geography" moves him across a larger expanse. Thomas invokes longitude and latitude, as well as the names of even the smallest Ontario hamlets (some in footnotes), all bird's-eye points of view to chart Thomas, Katarina and Mr. Mataf's progress across southern Ontario; the concomitant decline of the adults' relationship; and the tentative beginnings of Thomas's relationship to his mother. The section's overview is contrasted with the child's perspective, typically from the backseat of the car, from where Thomas attempts to gauge the status of his human environment.

"For a frightened child, I was self-possessed," Thomas comments when, on the first night of the journey, he is relegated to the back seat of the car while Katarina and Mr. Mataf sleep in a tent. As in the first two parts of the novel, the narrator employs subsections to interrogate his experience. For example, in "Hunger, " he first muses over his (adult) pleasure in not eating until his body begins to consume itself. He then relates, reproducing Thomas, the child's point of view, how Katarina and Mr. Mataf, virtually penniless, used him as decoy to steal food from a grocery store. After instructing him to steal, they helped the shopkeeper to catch him while Katarina stuffed food into her purse.

> From here, it looks unfair; a humiliation I could have done without. Though, when I try to imagine a better plan, I see both her point and her daring...[Now] I rarely do what anyone asks me to do without scrupulously thinking it over...I do not think my mother had any of this in mind when she slapped me [in front of the store owner], but, all the same, her slap is an enduring caution" (104-105).

As in his descriptions of his life with his grandmother, Thomas recalls what must be deeply upsetting events dispassionately. Later, abandoned at the side of the road by Mr. Mataf, Thomas and his mother walk to Ottawa. Thomas says he recalls little of this journey, mentioning only Katarina's silence. This he interprets as covering her desperate reflections on how to avoid their destination, Henry Wing's doorstep.

Their arrival in Ottawa opens the novel's third section, "The Sciences." Its epigram is a partial list of the sciences of divination. Henry Wing is, Thomas tells us, "a Black man with Chinese blood, handsome, tall, forty years old, in love with a woman eleven years younger, at work on an encyclopedia of limited appeal, living on Cooper Street in the city of my dreams, my father perhaps. Considerate is the word for him, considerate and loving" (137).

Katarina's ambivalence about Henry is as inexplicable to Thomas as everything else in his life. With respect to *Childhood*'s racial subtext, Henry Wing is a crucial figure.

In *Childhood*, only in Henry's house are the inhabitants described in terms of their Blackness. When Katarina and Thomas arrive, the door is opened by "a dark old woman with red hair," and the house smells of "exotic cooking." On first sight, Thomas notes that Henry Wing has "skin as dark as my mother's." In this shabby Victorian house, whose owner remains resolutely nineteenth-century in outlook and sensibility, the Black body is named, safe, and so the significance of race in the context of the nation can be explored, at least by implication.

Central to this exploration is Mrs. Williams, Henry Wing's housekeeper, who presides over Henry Wing's home and table. Of all the characters in *Childhood*, only she speaks in the Trinidadian vernacular, tells Caribbean stories, cooks Caribbean food. Only by Mrs. Williams does Thomas truly feel fed: "It's strange, now that I think of it, how easily I accepted as much of Mrs. Williams cooking as I did." Thomas observes:

> It was mostly Caribbean and, until I discovered Henry's Trinidadian descent, inexplicably foreign. Yet, I took to plantain and roti, dasheen and doubles as if I were born to them...Not that Henry's home was Caribbean. It wasn't, but it was more so than anything I'd known. My grandmother, after all, had swept Trinidad from her own life and surroundings. Here, in this household, buljol and sugar cake belonged" (139).

Thomas observes: "Henry seemed to have almost equal affection for Mrs. Williams and my mother" (143). It is not surprising, then, that Katarina soon has Henry dismiss Mrs. Williams, implicating Thomas in her accusations that Mrs. Williams had stolen her shoes. Thomas speculates that Mrs. Williams, and the "Caribbean aspect" she brought to Henry's home reminded his mother of her childhood, wondering if his grandmother had, when Kata was young, been less "diligent in hiding her origins." Katarina's attack on Mrs. Williams, then, apparently motivated by jealousy, repeats Edna's vehement but unexplained denial and discarding of her own ethnicity. Concerning his mother's treatment of Mrs. Williams, Thomas concludes: "I can't think of her behaviour without remembering how little I understood it" (139). Of his own role, and Henry's, he reports feeling that they had been, somehow, "unfaithful" to Mrs. Williams. The unfaithfulness resides in the narrative as well, for Thomas exhibits no interest in who Mrs. Williams might have been outside of Henry's home. Important to the novel's treatment of race, when Mrs. Williams is banished, so are racial markers from the text. Symbolically, the last time Thomas visits Henry, many years later, he notices that the house smells not "exotic" but of cooking cabbage. [9]

Henry is not Thomas's father (who he was, Thomas never discovers), but the present-day Thomas is, in many respects, his son. Obsessed by abstruse ideas, Henry Wing spends his life in solitary intellectual pursuits, moving between his magnificent library and his laboratory, all the while sustaining himself by wise investments. His major project is an encyclopedia of "unusual conceits"; his reading is prodigious. What he does in his laboratory is never exactly revealed, although he does teach Thomas chemistry, and once makes Thomas some gold. The alchemy is a trick, of course. This Thomas discovers when he insists on repeating it, and Henry tells him that he had purchased the gold in advance — a more benign and less complex hoax than Katarina's and Mr. Mataf's, but for Thomas, provides another caution. Henry's pursuit of knowledge is arcane, catholic, all consuming. Some of the novel's most affecting passages concern Henry's final systematic disassembling of his library into apparently random piles around the house which, he explains to Thomas, represent the degree to which a book will help him discover a cure for cancer. Only later does Thomas realize that this disassembling coincides with Katarina's fatal illness, of which he, and perhaps Henry as well, are unaware.

Orphaned at the early age of seven, Henry had been sent to Canada to work for a distant cousin, whose name he later took. His had been a lonely childhood, for he worked in his cousin's store constantly; reading his only recreation. How he first met Katarina, we are never told. Despite his insistence that he knows Henry well, Thomas reflects:

Why would a twentieth-century man, Trinidadian at that, choose to live in a Victorian setting, with a gentleman's lab, old-fashioned books, and courtly attitudes that would have marked him as "stuffy" centuries ago?

I have sometimes thought Henry misguided or eccentric. I've thought him laughable or bizarre, all depending on my distances from him: temporal, physical, or psychological. Lately, though I see in him another version of my grandmother.

They had different personalities, of course, but my grandmother's fanatic attachment to Lampman and Dickens, her disapproval of anything that might link her to Trinidad...these things had their echo in Henry...

You'd think Henry would hold on to the Trinidad of his early happiness, but I suppose any version of the island brought with it the painful memory of abandonment. Canada, his new home, must have seemed vague and impersonal, if only because what he knew best was the inside of a small shop in Sandy Hill, not much to go on and too little to love. And so, as I see it, he took such part of world and time as he found appealing in the books he loved (168-169).

A subject of Thomas's inquiry, then, is the relation of race and place. In Thomas's account, his grandmother and Henry turn their back on Trinidad: Henry, because it is the scene of loss; Edna, inexplicably. In fact, however, Henry does not turn his back on Trinidad — though he does not return there — rather, he recreates it. The presence of Mrs. Williams in his home, until she is banished at Katarina's insistence, metonymically retains, the flavour and sound of his origins; in some respects his home is a colonial enclave, and he — a mimic man — his embrace of colonial culture seemingly absolute and frozen in time. The only occasions on which Henry leaves his house are related to the alchemy project; we have no sense at all that he lives in the world outside the house, although he certainly lives off the gains of world capital.

As a man of means and independent scholar, Henry Wing performs the perfect colonial mimicry, albeit of a form of colonial presence long past.[10] However, in his close relation with Mrs. Williams, Henry disrupts his own mimic posture. Significantly, it is Katarina who insists that his gaze be only on her, the born-here daughter of a woman who turned her back on Trinidad. This aspect of the novel is multivalent; into Edna's rejection, Thomas has no insight at all. Her cultural attachments are those of the school teacher's more limited learning; nonetheless, in her love of Lampman and Dickens, she projects a vision of herself as having escaped her origins. Yet, as Thomas records, she habitually wore two dresses, both in the colours of the Trinidadian flag, a fact he insists is incidental.

If Mrs. Williams comprises the presence of the Caribbean in *Childhood*, its meaning is mired in class. Mrs. Williams is uneducated and education leaves her in awe. In *Childhood*, then, poverty and ignorance are as inextricably tied to Caribbean ethnicity as are stories, maubry and ginger beer — upward mobility requires discarding its marks and practices. What cannot be discarded, however, is the Black body, which, like the flag that Edna disavows yet wears everywhere, remains an insistent presence. Thomas's comment that Mrs. William's cooking ceased to be exotic when he discovered Henry's Caribbean origin is significant. Within the Canadian context, "Caribbeanness" — a homogenization of what is otherwise a diverse location — provides context for, and so legitimates, Black bodies in Canada while simultaneously marking them as foreign.[11]

In *Childhood*'s conclusion, Thomas remarks, "After all, I come from somewhere." What evokes this sense of genealogy is strange, however. His loved one steps off a curb and he pulls her back from the traffic. Years before, his grandfather had similarly stepped off a curb while in conversation with his grandmother, and had been hit by a car and killed. If genealogy is repetition with difference, in *Childhood*'s terms, what is the pattern, and what is difference? One difference is, of course, the Canadianization of Black bodies, the exchange of Caribbean context and place for that of Canada. If Thomas is the product of that exchange, he neither understands its meaning nor sees in it any possibility. By its title, "Housecleaning," that final chapter, erases the links to elsewhere, but replaces them is unclear. Tellingly, Thomas observes – in a memory projection — that the smell of Henry's favorite soap still lingers in the house.

Ironically, given Alexis's discomfort with things African-American, *Childhood*'s circular construction, as well as its conclusion, are somewhat reminiscent of that African-American classic, *Invisible Man*, Ralph Ellison's epic on the subversive meaning of the Black presence in the US republic. Just like Ellison's protagonist begins and concludes his narrative from his underground home beneath the streets of New York, Alexis's Thomas begins and concludes from his room in the Ottawa house that he has inherited from Henry. Where

Ellison's narrator closes with the promise that eventually he will emerge from hibernation, Thomas concludes, "I am able to wait, not without anxiety or sadness, but rather, like Henry, in the hope that...with the faith that...Whatever it is time brings" (265).

However, the differences between the two works may clarify what emerges from a reading of race in *Childhood*. Ellison's unnamed hero is driven underground by cataclysmic events in which he played a significant role, both as victim and as agent in history. In contrast, Alexis's protagonist requires a schedule to turn his activities into events that can be noticed. His philosophical stance is born of estrangement rather than engagement. Read as a story of a Canadian childhood, it records a life from which no meaning can be gleaned. Yet, the protagonist insists it is "singular" — not generic or representative. This statement suggests that it is neither Richard Wright's *Black Boy*, that is, representative of the racial group to which the protagonist belongs, nor unique in the sense that all lives are distinctive. In what sense, then, is it singular?

One way in which it is singular is in its difference from anything that normalizes. In the section marked "History," Thomas describes the family lives of his various neighbours in some detail, the kind of detail observed by a child whose home situation is "not normal." Two families are nuclear, and one is single-parent, but all nurture in the ordinary ways in which families are supposed to. In "Geography," Thomas, with his Black mother and her francophone partner, make their way across southern Ontario, that bastion of Anglo-Canadian culture. Their progress across the map is the section's principal concern, settling is out of the question, yet arriving is also at question, not only because Katarina and Mr. Mataf's relationship is disintegrating but also because the car, in need of a new radiator, is an uncertain conveyance. Life at Henry's is anything but "normal." When Thomas and Katarina first arrive, Henry's parlour is filled with bejewelled and perfumed women, whom he dismisses in honour of their arrival. The women, Thomas tells us, were probably men, commenting that while neither transvestite nor homosexual himself, Henry enjoyed their company because, he said, it kept him faithful to Kata. Besides, he explains to Thomas at one point, "It was good to be reminded of women in the company of men." Thus, nothing in Thomas's life occupied the "normal."

How are we to read *Childhood* in terms of Alexis's desire to articulate the nation? In "Housecleaning," we are told that Katarina moved back to her mother's house in Petrolia, and lived there quietly for a number of years before her somewhat premature death from cancer. In the same section, Thomas provides the bare outlines of his own similarly unremarkable life in the nearly two decades prior to his mother and Henry's deaths. Although he occupies Henry's house, nothing of its specificity remains. In his single return trip to Petrolia — to visit, and then to bury, his mother — he visits Mr. Goodman, who praises him, saying his own children never visit any more. Racism has apparently disappeared. His Black body, and that of his mother, even in Petrolia, seem to have no significance. *Childhood* seems to suggest that once the markers of the Caribbean are discarded or repressed, race is of no consequence in the Canadian landscape. Its narrator, however, writes from within a small room, to a lover he has yet to invite to his house, her arrival endlessly deferred by the novel's concluding commitment to passivity. *Childhood* is a work of obsessive and recursive self-articulation, suggesting that, at this point in time, neither can the narrator articulate the nation, nor is the nation prepared to articulate him.

In her introduction to *Frontiers*, entitled "Echoes in a Stranger Land," Nourbese Philip employs two daring terms to record and deconstruct the problem of the relation to the nation for Black people in Canada. "M/Othering" and "Be/longing" comprise her focus. Using the orthography of the postmodern statement, both terms are bifurcated to display tensions and (im)possibilities. The first term addresses the need of the descendents of African slaves, initially "othered" as a condition of their servitude, and then by a persistent attitude toward their race. Philip boldly figures the reversal of that relation with the addition of a single initial consonant, the new word signalling the most intense form of intimate human relation and need. The need to m/other and be mothered is mutual, she suggests; the nation needs to embrace all those it has abused, and the "othered" need to be embraced and included. The second term, be/longing, is similarly bold. In terms of the essay, its play is multiple, insisting on the "being here" of Native peoples, Africans and Asians — indeed, all who now have "long" inhabited the New World. "Be/longing" expresses the human desire to "belong," where one is "long" yet the longing to be/long is disturbed, ruptured by the virgule's division that signals impossibility, similarly reflected in the m/other that is not (yet).

As gloss for *Childhood*, Philips's terms are uncanny: the novel virtually enacts them. Longing, or love, is the narrator's stated subject, yet the only unabashed and unrestrained longing that *Childhood*'s narrator observes is that of Henry for Katarina, his mother. His own longings are unexpressed, only obliquely self-acknowledged, yet each of the novel's four divisions may be said to concern themselves solely with these unmentioned issues. In *Childhood*, there are no mothers; belonging is achieved only by the repression of longing; and the equilibrium with which the novel concludes is achieved only by desire deferred.

Work Cited

Alexis, André. *Childhood*. Toronto: McCelland & Stewart, 1998

_____. "Borrowed Blackness." *This Magazine*. May 1995:14-20.

_____. "Crossroads: seeing art as politics ought to make it controversial: then why is it so easy to ignore?." *This Magazine*. March-April, 1997 : 30-35

_____. "Taking a Swipe at Canada," *Globe and Mail*, January 7, 1995: C19.

_____. *Despair and Other Stories of Ottawa*. Toronto: Coach House Press, 1994. Rpt. McCelland & Stewart, 1998.

Bhabha, Homi. *The Location of Culture*. New York: Routledge. 1994.

The Concise Oxford Dictionary of Current English, Sixth edition. Oxford: Clarendon Press, 1976.

Gorjup, Branko. "From despair to childhood: Branko Gorjup speaks with André Alexis." *Books Canada*, 27(3) April 1998: 11-14.

Mercer, Kobena. "Witness at the Crossroads: An Artist's Journey in Post-colonial Space." In Keith Piper: *Relocating the Remains*. London: Institute of International Visual Arts, 1997.

Nurse, Donna. "Somewhere man: in *Childhood*, André Alexis finds meaning in absence, belonging and place." *Quill and Quire*. 64(3) March 1998: 1,10.

Philip, M. Nourbese. *Frontiers: essays and writings on Racism and Culture*. Stratford: Mercury Press, 1992.

Redhill, Michael. "An Interview with André Alexis." *Brick: a literary journal*. No.62, Spring 1999: 50-57.

Wright, Richard. *Black Boy*. New York: Perennial Classics, 1998.

Endnotes

1. Dionne Brand, from whose point of view, in his review, Alexis disassociates himself, later won the Governor General's Award for Poetry, Canada's most prestigious literary prize. Moreover, *Bread Out of Stone* was extremely well received, and has recently been reissued. The reception of Dionne Brand's work by the Canadian literary establishment comprises another narrative of "reading" and "race" in Canada. It is not necessarily a counter-narrative to that of Alexis; in fact, she is now widely acclaimed but still not, in the main, intelligently reviewed.

2. "If the novel is about love and origin, and the origin is a mystery, "Alexis commented to Michael Redhill, "the race of the child has to be a mystery…it's something that is discovered, that is a surprise within the narrative itself."

3. The phrase is taken from the title of a 1993 book by the African American philosopher Cornel West.

4. Elsewhere in her interview, Donna Nurse writes: "Although he couldn't have been more than two or three at the time, Alexis, now forty-one,can still remember the trauma of an absence, and the perplexity of his family's reunion in Ottawa in 1961 when he was four years old. "It was hurtful in the sense that I was old enough to know that my parents were gone and not conscious enough to know there was a good reason for it…By the time I came to meet them I didn't know them anymore…" Alexis's experience is not uncommon among people from the Caribbean. Other writers have focussed on it directly, notably M. Nourbese Philip, *Harriet's Daughter* (Toronto: Women's Press, 1988) and Cecil Foster, *Sleep On, Beloved* (Toronto: Random House, 1995).

5. A vampire-like figure in Trinidadian folktales.

6. The word "discipline" in its various first meanings is suggestive: "1. Branch of instruction or learning; mental and moral training, adversity as effecting this; system or rules for conduct; behaviour according to established rules."

7. In its abundance of allusion and devices such as repetition, *Childhood* may be called postmodern, although Alexis vehemently rejects this label.

8. This scrutiny of nature as diversion from the narrator's childhood unhappiness is strongly reminiscent of two passages in *Black Boy*, the African American writer Richard Wright's story of his own painful childhood (7-8, 45-46).

9. It certainly is possible to read the cooking motif in *Childhood* as conventional multicultural associations of ethnicity with food, and other distinctive practices, and so to see the dismissal of Mrs. Williams as a rejection of the traces of origin, the immigrant, and the legitimacy of immigrant voices. Given Alexis's public statements, this reading is plausible. However, if Mrs. Williams is read symbolically and metonymically, I think that a more disturbed and problematic reading of *Childhood* emerges with respect to race. For example, it has been suggested to me by Rinaldo Walcott that Mrs. William's yellow headscarf is not ordinary Caribbean dress, but rather a fixture of the Mammy figure with which Mrs. Williams can readily be associated. North American Black stereotypes, then, may be said to intrude upon this text, despite the author's desire to evade and avoid African American associations.

10. Homi Bhabha understands the mimicry of the colonial as essentially repetition with difference; similarity to the colonizer, is itself a sign of subversiveness, rendering the colonial incapable of being known.

11. Hazelle Palmer's anthology, "*— But where are you really from?*": *Stories about Identity and Assimilation in Canada* (Toronto: Sister Vision, 1997) focuses on the endemic experience of Black Canadians of finding themselves always perceived as from "elsewhere" no matter how many generations ago their ancestors moved to Canada.

The Last Days of Blackness:
André Alexis Gets Over

Peter Hudson

Following a certain logic of assimilation in Canada, André Alexis's *Childhood* is arguably the legitimate textual successor to the so-called immigrant narratives of Austin Clarke's Toronto Trilogy.[1] Clarke's novels famously distilled the experiences of Caribbean migrants who settled and sojourned in Canada in the post-War era. The history of Black people and Black literature in Canada predates his writing, but whether or not we have read his work, they have become a part of the foundational myths of Black Canadian history. With his depiction of an encounter with a hostile and frozen Canadian landscape, the experience of Clarke's characters replicates that of other immigrant groups. The crucial difference, of course, is the presence of a peculiarly Canadian anti-Black racism, and the fact that the Caribbean looms large in Clarke's novels, providing a refuge from the cultural and geographical space of Canada.

Childhood, however, is marked by the ambivalence of second or third generation Black Canadians — the children and grandchildren of Clarke's generation — whose ties to the Caribbean have been eroded by an immersion in Canadian life and many of whom accept at face value Canada's optimistic rhetoric of multiculturalism and inclusivity. In many ways it is a rebellious text. Alexis disturbs the complacent equilibrium of the Black middle class in Canada, not through a radical critique of racism or a righteous, incendiary form of anger, but through a kind of Black bourgeois degeneracy that bears witness to an abandonment of faith in the name of accoutrements of suburban respectability: cotillions, beauty pageants, award ceremonies, professional ambitions, and Cecil Foster novels. This is not, however, the artless drivel of Lawrence Brathwaite's *Wigger*, with its cheap and gratuitous pornography — though Alexis shares much of Brathwaite's irony — but a rebellion on a more benign level. Through an apparent turning away from the normative modes of Blackness that have remained hegemonic despite the de rigeur rhetoric of hybridity, difference, and anti-essentialism within postcolonial studies, *Childhood* narrates an anti-aesthetic of the normative ontologies of Blackness in Canada. In other words, it is the novel of a phenotypically Black man who, for all intents and purposes, is white.

I don't say this to dismiss *Childhood*: for this very reason it is an important, if also a disturbingly difficult — and problematic — text. I, for one, am happy to see a Black author refuse a programmatic relationship to the Caribbean (and for that matter, to refuse the afro-pastoral spaces that make up another vector of the romantic Black Canadian narrative). To his credit, Alexis is able to free himself from the rhetorical shackles of a fiction motivated by the dogmatic necessities of identity politics and the search for an authentic, oppositional, distinctively "Black" voice. *Childhood* does contain the narcissistic interrogations of the self that mark the fiction of identity, but his skills as a writer grant him a degree of subtlety often lacking in this kind of work. Where the novel falters, and where it might have learned from the polemical engagements of the "race" or "protest" novel, is in its inability to revise and critique many of the stereotypes and caricatures of Black people that have plagued white representations of Blacks.

Set in Ottawa and the southern Ontario town of Petrolia, *Childhood* is Thomas MacMillan's hesitant attempt to recount and make sense of a childhood marked by neglect and abandonment. A present-day technician in an Ottawa laboratory, MacMillan, who shares the same birth date with the author (though Alexis insists the work is not autobiographical) writes to an elusive "you," apparently a lover. He never knew his father; and his mother, Katarina, deposits him with Edna, his embittered and abusive grandmother in Petrolia. Katarina returns for Thomas when he is ten, soon after Edna's death, and whisks him away to Ottawa where they stay with a kindly but eccentric Chinese-Trinidadian, Henry Wing. Until Katarina tires of his devotion, Wing becomes the closest thing to a father that Thomas has known, and indeed, whether or not he actually is his father remains one of *Childhood's* enduring, unresolved mysteries. For

Thomas, the provisional nuclear family he finds with Katarina and Wing is central to his emotional development, and it becomes central to his interrogation of his own self. "I might even have said my early childhood was good, if I hadn't decided to write it, to write about the others who populated it," comments MacMillan in the quotation that would become, in absence of an author's endorsement, the back-cover blurb. "There's nothing to be done, though. The way to Katarina and Henry is through me" (29).

As a narrator, MacMillan is detached, almost autistic. The neglect he has received has made him into an obsessive positivist whose craving for order obliterates any sense of spontaneity or passion. As a child, he is attracted to the meticulous ordering and classification of the scientific disciplines; as an adult, he becomes a compulsive list maker. The novel is often broken up by lists of everything from the curses of one of Katarina's lovers to minute-by-minute breakdowns of Thomas's daily routine.

The representation of MacMillan's anomic personality is aided by Alexis's parse, restrained writing. Other than Alexis's repeated, sloppy use of the ellipsis, which becomes a kind of annoying writer's tick ("And yet..." (215) and "And so on..." (22) appear to be his favourite phrases, apparently suggesting an unspoken insight), *Childhood* is economically written. Too, for Alexis, English is not, to use Marlene Nourbese Philips's phrase, a "foreign anguish." [2] His writing implicitly refuses arguments for the inadequacy of English to carry the Black experience. He thus rejects the valorization of the demotic as an instrument capable of performing the Black cultural difference proposed by Black cultural nationalists, and his writing marks an attempt to revise the geography of Black Canadian letters by refusing its supposed exceptionalism — its essential cultural or formal difference from the wider Canadian canon. Black Canadian writing, Alexis seems to suggest, simply does not — cannot — exist, since the Black Canadian experience is essentially no different than that of other Canadians.

Still, the text does seem haunted by an undisclosed trauma of colonialism and the dislocations of immigration. Of his grandmother Edna, MacMillan says: "Her life, but for the years in Trinidad, was lived in Petrolia, and Petrolia crushed everything from her so thoroughly that I could not have guessed her origins were anything but Canadian" (29). In a footnoted non sequitur he adds:

It's true that the flag of Trinidad is the same red, white, and Black as my grandmother's dresses, but that was a coincidence, I think. The island gained its independence in 1962, long after she'd left it, long after it had ceased to matter to her (29).

What it was in Petrolia that "crushed everything from her so thoroughly" or why Trinidad — her past — had "ceased to matter to her," Alexis doesn't explain. Undoubtedly, the loss of her husband, whom Thomas is named after, suddenly killed crossing the street a step ahead of her, had had something to do with it. "Edna MacMillan must certainly have gone through hell watching the man she loved die on the street," comments Alexis. "It may even have driven her to more excessive drink or begun a rift between her and her daughter" (37). But he admits that "all this is just modest guessing," and later in the novel MacMillan reveals that Edna's disinterest in Trinidad was not simply a benign eclipsing of memory but a "diligent" effort "in hiding her origins" (139). Hence, what, presumably, ignited the engine of assimilation that accounted for the "inexplicably foreign" (139) nature of Caribbean food to the young Thomas. Edna appears marked by a colonial taint that impels her to identify with English culture. Indeed, Alexis describes Edna's attempts to ingratiate herself to the Dickens Society of Lambton County which disintegrated after Edna slapped a women across the face because she disagreed with her opinion.

Instead of pursuing these larger questions of culture and colonialism, however, Alexis interrogates the micro-politics of the personal. Here, again, his restrained prose serves him well. His minimalist style allows the reader to witness the unfolding of the ironies and little tragedies that seem to make up MacMillan's life, thankfully sparing us the intrusive, overly analytic editorializing narrator. The most profound example occurs during Thomas's second year in university, after he has left home. Thomas is beginning to be able to see Katarina not only as a mother but as a social entity — "Katarina" — unto herself. They meet for lunch and end up discussing "the latest man to disappoint her," "Erwin Lewis, a Jamaican whose accent I never managed to decipher" (220). "I don't remember how Erwin came up," comments Thomas. "How long had he been gone? Why had he left? How could he be so cruel? It all struck me as pointless" (220). Emboldened, perhaps, by his recently found independence, and irritated by having to meet her at lunch, thus breaking his normal routine, he begins a flippant interrogation of her.

— Why do you get involved with men like that? I asked.
— What should I do? she asked, smiling.
— You should be sensible. The way it looks to me, you like being miserable...
(That was a good one)
— I don't have any sympathy for you, I said.
And I told her why. She hated herself. She was irresponsible. She lacked consideration. Moved by my own rhetoric, I made a variety of suggestions, from psychoanalysis (for her) to self-restraint. And it seemed to me we were finally communicating, that I was telling her things she hadn't heard (220).

It's a brutally honest moment in the novel. His words are dishearteningly reckless and cruel, the more so, it seems, because of MacMillan's utter inability to monitor the impact of them on others.

I didn't believe in psychoanalysis then. I don't believe in it now. It's no more than testicle scratching, but I suggested it because it sounded adult, and I remember talking on and on, looking up to see her smiling face, taking her smile for encouragement.
And then I looked up and she was crying. How long had she been crying?
— Did I say something wrong?
— No, Thomas... I'm sorry.
She took a handkerchief from the sleeve of her jacket, took off her glasses to wipe her eyes.
— I thought you didn't love Erwin?
— But I don't...
— Why can't you be honest?
(Another good one.)
— What are you crying about?
— I don't know.
That put an end to the conversation. Her eyes were puffed up, her hands unsteady. Sniffling, she rooted in her purse for a compact mirror and make-up. She was thirty-nine, younger than I am now, but she seemed impossibly old.

And I was resentful, at first, because I thought: This has something to do with me… but I was only trying to be helpful. It's her fault for being so sensitive. She didn't have the right to take my words so seriously, She's never done that before.

It was as if she'd betrayed me (221).

It's this distance that also allows Alexis one of the simplest, yet profoundest insights into a very particular form of Canadian racism. At one point in the novel, MacMillan describes "the only conflict" that he had with his first girlfriend, Margaret Goodman. They are watching "Woody Woodpecker" in the Goodmans's basement when a friend, Darren McGuinness says, "in his usual friendly way,"

— Here nigger nigger nigger…
— He's not a nigger, she said.

That brought such mirth from those around us, I wasn't sure whether I should laugh or not. When Margaret ran out to the yard, I didn't know if I should follow or stay in the basement with the others.

I did follow her out, but I was upset that she'd ruined my afternoon (62).

Similar to that peculiar liberal fallacy of "s/he's not like other Blacks," Margaret's defense of Thomas — "He's not a nigger" — acts to legitimize the speech act by arguing for Thomas's exceptionalism and implicitly suggesting that other Black people are, in fact, niggers, with all the baggage that word carries.

The incident recalls, though with almost opposite effect, Frantz Fanon's encounter on the streets of Paris with a child who points to him and turns to his mother exclaiming, "Look, a negro!"[3] For Fanon, the moment unleashes an interior dialogue on the ontology of Blackness and the racial politics of colonialism. Alexis dismisses the incident with an ironic shrug. Granted, what other defenses could a child have? I'm unsure if there is a proper authorial intervention that could redeem the situation without destroying the novel's fragile psychological architecture, a response that wouldn't be out of character with MacMillan as narrator. As well, it is the ambivalence of fiction — without the dominance of one single narrative voice — that makes such a complex moment possible. And indeed, if we turn to Alexis's journalistic, non-fiction pieces, what emerges is a conservative, almost reactionary response to questions of race, that is masked in a kind of rational liberalism whose condescending tone suggests that, not only is Canada not so bad, but that to discuss racism or to link oneself with Black struggles is reactionary and an act of cultural appropriation.[4] (Alexis's use of Irving Layton and Osip Mandelstam are not, of course.) So it becomes another atomized moment in the book, another point in the catalogue of MacMillan's experience, as meaningless, ambiguous, and insignificant as any other, adding to the curiously unfinished feeling that the book has; it's unsettling lack of closure.

In some places, however, the ironic mask that allow Alexis the ability for such a subtle commentary on the politics of race — which allows him to move beyond race as the prime motivator of the narrative — begins to slip. Occasionally, the book is disappointing in its uncritical and unimaginative reinscriptions of racist stereotypes. The most jarring example of this is the figure of Mrs. Williams, the maid of Henry Wing's house who is Katarina's unpleasant embodiment of the Caribbean. Yet Mrs. Williams signifies less a Caribbean entity, than the mammy figure of early twentieth-century American racist mythology.[5] An illiterate, handkerchief-wearing Jamaican woman, whom Thomas first sees "shuffl[ing] amiably" into the dining room (138). In fact, shuffling seems to be her only mode of walking. "She would sometimes shuffle into the library," comments MacMillan on page 141, "dust rag in hand, and watch me read, something she couldn't do herself." And later: "I vividly remember Mrs. Williams from these last moments: impassive, silent, a little frail, shuffling, head bowed, shoes clacking noisily on the floor" (157). Her speech comes out in a half-baked pidgin, reminiscent of that spoken by Black characters of the Plantation literature of the Reconstruction South: "Mr. Wing, you know I does never freeze anything," she says at one point. "I have some okra and rice in the fridge." (138)

Here too, the portrayal of Mrs. Williams contains a measure of ambivalence, as it is often unclear whether her portrayal is a result of the limited vocabularies of Thomas-as-child-narrator, or that of Alexis-as-author. Either way, however, it's a departure from Alexis's studied approach to character; and beneath Mrs. Williams's mammy surface, little personality emerges. She has a catalytic function in the book; however, it is one that rehearses the relations between the plantation mistress and her female servants.[6] Mrs. Williams and Katarina become involved in a power struggle for a semblance of control of the house and for the attention of its master, Mr. Wing, with MacMillan musing that perhaps "in her own way, Mrs. Williams was in love with Henry" (155). It begins with Katarina's injunction against the use of Scotch bonnet peppers in Mrs. Williams's rice and peas and eventually escalates to the point where Henry dismisses Mrs. Williams over a sartorial scandal. In order to get Mrs. Williams fired, Katarina compels Thomas to lie, suggesting that he saw Mrs. Williams stealing Katarina's shoes.

It is, perhaps, a small incident, but it's a curious one in a novel that is so controlled, so meticulous in its construction of character and its ordering of the mildly chaotic unreliability of the narrator's memory. *Childhood* is, at times, almost brilliant in its attempts to write with the kind of literary freedom that lifts the burden of representation that Black authors inevitably seem to shoulder. But at what cost? By refusing that burden, Alexis unwittingly grafts himself onto a Canadian discourse where Blackness has already been so thoroughly inscribed and overwritten as to make it almost invisible in its effects, its powerfully dehumanizing racism a part of everyday Canadian life. Regretfully, this is the Canada that Alexis vaunts, even while it is the kind of Canada that he, paradoxically, refuses to admit exists.

Endnotes

1. André Alexis, *Childhood*, (Toronto: McClelland and Stewart, 1998).

2. *She Tries Her Tongue Her Silence Softly Breaks.* (Charlottetown, P.E.I: Ragweed Press, 1989), 53.

3. Frantz Fanon, *Black Skin, White Masks.*, (Charles Lam Markmann, Trans. New York: Grove Press, 1967), 109.

4. See, for instance, André Alexis, "Borrowed Blackness." *This Magazine*, May 1995, vol. 28, no. 8, p. 14-20; and his review of Dionne Brand's *Bread out of Stone*, "Taking a swipe at Canada," *The Globe and Mail*, Jan. 7, 1995, C19. Rinaldo Walcott points out that "it would be silly to be offended by André Alexis suggesting, in *This Magazine*, that Blackness in Canada is 'borrowed,' Blackness is always

borrowed." See "Scattered Speculations on Canadian Blackness; Or, Grammar for Black," *Black Like Who?: Writing Black Canada*, (Toronto: Insomniac Press, 1991), 134. Indeed, while I cannot, unfortunately, go into his detailed analysis of his essays here, it would be silly to be offended, or take seriously, almost any of Alexis's journalistic prose.

5. I am grateful to Rinaldo Walcott for drawing this point to my attention.

6. See, for instance the section "Dressed to Kill" in Joan Dayan's *Haiti, History, and the Gods*, (Berkeley, CA: University of California Press, 1998), 170-180.

Contributor's Biographies

Richard Almonte is a Ph.D. student in the English Department at McMaster University.

Tess Chakkalakal is a Ph.D. student in the English Department at York University. She has been a visiting scholar at the Center for Cultural Studies, University of North Carolina, Chapel Hill.

Peter Hudson is a writer and critic. He is finishing his MA in Interdisciplinary Studies at York University.

Awad El Karim M. Ibrahim is Assistant Professor of Education at the University of Ottawa.

Joy Mannette is Associate Professor in the Faculty of Education, York University. She is the editor of *Elusive Justice: Beyond the Marshall Enquiry* (1992).

David Sealy is a writer, lecturer and philosopher. He lives and writes in Nova Scotia.

Gamal Abdel Shehid is Assistant Professor in the Faculty of Psychical Education, University of Alberta. He is currently working on a book on race, masculinity, nation and sport.

Renuka Sooknanan is finishing her Ph.D. in the Sociology Department at York Univeristy. She is writing a dissertation on the problems of community activism. She is also a member of the Fuse editorial board.

Leslie Sanders is Associate Professor of Humanities, Atkinson College, York University. She is the author of *The Development of Black Theatre in America: From Shadows to Selves* (1988).

Rinaldo Walcott is Assistant Professor of Humanities at York University. He is the author of *Black Like Who? Writing Black Canada* (1997).

Index

Note: Page locators in **boldface** point to bibliographic references found in end-of-chapter Works Cited lists. Locators containing the letter *n* (eg., 136n11) refer to persons and/or concepts cited in an endnote.

Artz, Sybille, 162
Asante, Molefi, 91
Aubert de Gaspé, Philippe, 21-23, **24**
Austin, J.L., 163, 165

Bailey, Donovan, 71
Ball, Ian, 166
Bannerji, Himani, 145
Banning, Kass, 99
Baptiste, Jean, 63
Barnes Collection, 141
baseball, 79-81
basketball, 129
Battiste, Marie, 62
Bearden, Jim, **46**
Beaton, Elizabeth, 61
becoming, 111
    vs. being, 114
becoming Black, 111-33
Bernard, Delvina, 59, 60
Bhabha, Homi, 15, 32-33, 37, **46**, 112, 118, **133**, **185**, 187n10
Bibb, Henry, 34
Bills of Indenture, 56-57
biology, as a way of relating to Blackness, 125
Black Abolitionist Papers, The, 33-34, **47**
Black Atlantic (Gilroy), 40, **47**, 106n26, 130, **133**
Black Boy (Wright), 183, **185**, 187n8
Black Canadians
    absence from Black history, 40-42, 44, 59
    community among, 45, 139-40
    culture loss, 89-91, 102-3, 125-28, 182
    difference from Black Americans, 172
    diversity among, 30, 42-45, 140-43. *See also* difference
    identity, 91, 97
    imposition of African identity, 101-2
    in-between position, 32-33, 43
    place in the national imaginary, 30
    place in diasporic discourse, 31, 40-45, 91, 106n26
    political activity, 99, 102

Canada's place in, 40-42, **44**
Black Stylized English (BSE), 119, 125-28
Black Talk (Smitherman), 119, **135**
Black United Front, 59, 99
Blackness
    as "disruptive" element in Canadian society, 18, 20, 23-24, 37, 38, 82
    as a special effect, 38-39
    assimilation of, 182, 191
    in Canada, seen through American lens, 79
    Western representations of, 124
Boers, 66
border crossing, 34, 40-44, 46, 86n11, 91
borrowed Blackness, 21, 172
Bourdieu, Pierre, 122, **133**
Brady, Brad, 79
Brand, Dionne, **46**, 71, 81-83, **85**, 86n17, 171-72, 186n1, 198n4,
Brathwaite, Lawrence, 191-92
Bread Out of Stone (Brand), **85**, 171, 186n1, 198n4
Breaking the Ice (Sweeney), 45-46
Bristow, Peggy, 29, 30, **46**
Brown, Elsa Barkley, 38, **46**
Brunt, Stephen, 74
Bryant, Carolyn, 166
Burton, Antoinette, 41, **47**
Butler, Judith, 113, **133**, 161, 163-65,
Byrd, Donald, 106n26

cacaphony, 82-83
Callaghan, Morley, 14, 23-24, **24**
Canada, racism in, 35, 60, 64-66, 98-102, 114-18, 139-40, 167, 171,
    173, 191, 196-97
Canadian culture, death narrative, 71-72
Canadian identity
    incompatibility with Blackness, 98
    monocultural narrative, 77, 97-98
    myths surrounding, 60, 77, 99, 140
    speaking back to, 82
Canadian literature
    Black presence in, 13-14, 18-24

Haliburton, Thomas, 19-20, **25**
Halifax Citadel, 55
Halifax rules (hockey), 84
Hall, Stuart, 89, 92, 105n18, 120, **134**, 141
Hall, Thomas, 61
"Ham Hill", 166
Hamilton, Sherman, 71
Hamilton, Sylvia, **46**, 54, 60
Harriet's Daughter (Philip), **134**, 186n4
Heller, Monica, 123, **134**
Hill, Anita, 166
Hill, Daniel G., **47**
hip-hop, 119
history singing, 59
hockey
    Black players, 76-81
    constructionist view, 72-73
    death narrative, 71, 74-80, 82, 84
    mythology surrounding, 72-73
    parallels with political change, 72
    racism in, 76-78
    writing through race, 76-78
Hogan's Alley, 35
Home Game (Dryden & MacGregor), 73-75, **85**
homophobia, in hockey, 74-76
hooks, bell, 120, 132, **134**, 140n2,
Huckleberry Finn, 17
Hughes, Langston, 59

identity politics, 95-96, 129, 149
Imagined Communities (Anderson), **133**, 148-49,
immigrant guides, 16, 36
immigrants, and the third space, 112-13
Imperial Leather (McClintock), **47**
"In Praise of Talking Dogs" (Mount), 13, **25**
Indian Residential School, 55
Inoperative Community (Nancy), 151, 152-53
Into the Heart of Africa, 141
Invisible Man (Ellison), 182-83

Jackie Robinson (Rampersad), **85**, 86n12
Jackson, Lydia, 56
Jacobinism, 95
Jamaican immigrants, perceived as criminals, 100-101
James, C.E., 132, **134**
James, C.L.R., 91, 136n11
James, Graham, 76
Johnson, Albert, 100
Johnson, Eleanor, 62
Jones, Joan, 59
Jones, Rocky, 59, 99
Julien, Isaac, 145, 153
Just Desserts killing, 100-101

Kariya, Paul, 71
Kidd, Bruce, 73-76, **85**
Killing Rage (hooks), 140n2
Kipling, Rudyard, 23
Klein, Jeff, 74, **85**
knowledge
    common sense, 143-46
    rootedness of, 145
Kristeva, Julia, 111, **134**
Ku Klux Klan, 60, 100

language
    as symbolic capital, 121-22
    role in Black identity, 112
Language and Symbolic Power (Bourdieu), **133**
Lawrence, Eroll, 143-45, 155n8
Laws, Dudley, 101
Lawson, Guy, 161, 167
Lawson, Wade, 100
Layton, Irving, 197
Le Jeune, Olivier, 36
Lecker, Robert, 25n3
Les anciens Canadiens (Aubert de Gaspé), 14, 21-23, **24**
Life and Times of Mary Shadd Cary (Bearden & Butler), **46**
literary criticism, 14-16

Nova Scotia
Black cultural consciousness in, 59
Black exodus from, in 1791, 56-57
Black immigration to, 57-58
Black people abandoning since 1980s, 60
Black people in, 54-61
Nova Scotian identity, 60-61
Nurse, Donna, 174, 186n4, **185**

O'Ree, Willie, 79, 82, 86n11
Ogbu, John, **134**, 136n11
Oliver, William P., 61
one drop rule, 62
Open Ice conference, 74
otherness, 150-52

Padmore, George, 91
Palmer, Hazelle, 187n11
Pan-Africanism, 91
Pan Africanist Congress (PAC), 64, 67n4
Parks, Rosa, 59
paternalism, 172
Patterson, Orlando, 90, 102
Patterson, Steven, 63
pedagogy of the imaginary, 129-33
Pedagogy of the Oppressed (Freire), **133**
performativity, 112-13, 142, 149-50, 152, 163
desire and, 128-29
agency and, 113-14
performed subjectivity, 123-24
Performing the Postmodern (Walcott), **135**
Peters, Thomas, 56
Peterson, Carla, 33-34, 41, **47**
Philip, M. Nourbese, 89-91, 96-97, 102-3, 127, **134**, **185**, 186n4, 193,
Philosophical Discourse of Modernity, The (Habermas), 106n19
plain Canadian English, 127
Playing in the Dark (Morrison), 14, 16-17, **25**
Plea for Emigration, A (Shadd Cary), 16, **25**, 29, 30, 34, 36, **46**, **47**
plurivocality, 91-92. *See also* difference

popular culture
and language learning, 123
role in becoming Black, 119, 123-25
postcoloniality, 105n18
postmodernity, 94-96, 105n18
Preston (Nova Scotia), 54
Provincial Freeman, 29, 32, 43, 44-46
public gaze, 118, 130, 132

Quebecois literature, 21-23
Queen Latifah, 126

racial boundaries, transcending, 33-34
racial violence, 167
racism
in Canada, 35, 60, 64-66, 98-102, 114-18, 139-40, 167, 171, 173, 191, 196-97
in Canadian literature, 20-21, 23
in hockey, 76-78
rooted in common sense knowledge, 145
Rampersad, Arnold, **85**, 86n12
Ramphore, Sydney James Ramonametsi, 63-67
Rankin, John Morris, 61, 62
Rap City, 124, 136n9
rap
and learning of BESL, 125-28
choice of by young continental Africans, 130
female ambivalence toward, 127-28
influence on young continental African males, 125-27
rational subjectivity, 92-96, 106n19
exclusion of Black peoples, 93-95, 105n13
exclusion of women, 105n12
rationality, 93-94
real essence, 146
Reckless Eyeballing (Reed), 165-67
Redhill, Michael, 173, 186n2, **185**
Reed, Ishmael, 165-67
regulated visibility, 96-97
Reid-Pharr, Robert, 40, **47**